Surviving Your TODDLER

Surviving Your TODDLER

365 Creative Games and Activities to Help You Enjoy the Unique Challenges of Life with a One- to Three-Year-Old

TRISH KUFFNER

Lighthouse Books
1423 Dayton Street
Coquitlam, B.C. Canada
V3E 3H2

Cover and interior design by Ruth Linka
Cover illustrations by Sheila Manning Kinakin
Interior illustrations by Laurel Aiello

First printing, November, 1999

CANADIAN CATALOGUING IN PUBLICATION DATA

Kuffner, Patricia, 1960-
    Surviving your toddler

Includes index.
ISBN 0-9696626-2-9

1. Toddlers 2. Child rearing. 3. Parenting. 4. Amusements. I. Title.
HQ774.5.K84 1999   649'.5   C99-910727-5

Printed in Canada by Kromar Printing Ltd.

For Johanna, our toddler-in-residence.
Writing this book with you was difficult;
without you it would have been impossible.

▲ ◀ ▶ ◀ ▼ ▲

Table of Contents

Introduction 1

Chapter 1: Help! I Have a Toddler! 3
Organizing for a Toddler 5
Planning Your Activities 10
Stocking Your Craft Cupboard 11
What About Television? 13
A Word of Encouragement 14

Chapter 2: Rainy Day Play 15

Chapter 3: Kids in the Kitchen 53

Chapter 4: Water Play 65

Chapter 5: Outdoor Adventures 77

Chapter 6: Out and About 87

Chapter 7: Nursery Rhymes and Finger Plays 93

Chapter 8: Early Learning Fun 101

Chapter 9: Music and Movement 121

Chapter 10: Arts and Crafts 131
Scribbling and Drawing 133
Painting 138
Printmaking 152
Tearing, Gluing, and Sticking 156
Crafts and Other Fun Things to Make 163

Chapter 11: Birthday and Holiday Activities 169
Birthday Celebrations 170
Valentine's Day 173
St. Patrick's Day 176

Easter. 178
Canada Day. 181
Thanksgiving. 182
Halloween 185
Christmas 187
Hanukkah 195

Appendix A: Basic Craft Recipes. 199
Paint 199
Playdough. 203
Clay 205
Glue and Paste. 207
Other Craft Recipes 209

Appendix B: Crazy Can Activities 211

Appendix C: Best Toys for Babies and Toddlers. 212

Appendix D: Best Books for Babies and Toddlers 214

Appendix E: Resources. 219

Index. 222

Acknowledgements

WRITING A BOOK WHILE HOMESCHOOLING THREE CHILDREN, CHASING A TODDLER, and struggling through the early months of pregnancy was not an easy job, and one I could not have done without the help of some wonderful people.

First and foremost, I thank God for His love, mercy, and grace, for His leading in my life, and for the daily strength He gives me to meet the many challenges of parenting. I am sincerely thankful for my mother, Irene McGeorge, mother-in-law, Betty Kuffner, and friend, Joy Francescini, who have been so willing to care for my children when I needed time to write. I am so grateful for the help you have given me.

To my husband, Wayne, and our children, Andria, Emily, Joshua, and Johanna (Samuel, you weren't born yet!)—I thank you for being willing to put up with grilled-cheese-sandwich dinners, an absence of clean clothes, and Saturdays without Mom. I really appreciate the sacrifices you've made.

Thank you to Nancy Wise at Sandhill Book Marketing who ensures that my books are available in bookstores across the country. Your belief in and enthusiasm for self-publishing has encouraged me tremendously over the years. Without someone like you, self-publishers wouldn't stand a chance.

Finally, to my editors and the publisher of the U.S. version of this book, Leah Lev Oertel, Christine Zuchora-Walske, and Bruce Lansky at Meadowbrook Press, thank you for envisioning *Surviving Your Toddler* and giving me the opportunity to write it. Your support of my efforts inspires me to continue on this road called writing.

Introduction

Children are the anchors that hold a mother to life.

SOPHOCLES

I BEGAN WRITING *SURVIVING YOUR TODDLER* JUST AS MY FOURTH CHILD, Johanna, was entering the toddler stage. She began to walk, then run, several months short of her first birthday, and she hasn't stopped since! After surviving the baby/toddler/preschooler challenge three times with Johanna's older siblings, I'd forgotten what a trial one little toddler can be, especially the extremely active variety!

But what a joy, too, to watch her grow and develop through the various stages of toddlerhood. Before learning to crawl and walk, she was confined to sit wherever we put her, yet only months later she roamed the house at will. What a treat it was to watch her as she began to tease her siblings and mimic her parents, to see the beginnings of imaginative play as she cuddled her "baby," to notice the emerging concern she showed for others who were crying, and to observe the development of a giving spirit as she shared her cookie with the family cat!

Toddlerhood is a precious stage in the life of both parent and child, and one which can be enjoyed immensely if you are prepared to slow down a little, sit on the floor a lot, and worry about picking up the toys only when your child goes to bed at night. Organize your home to be a safe and interesting place for your child to explore and discover, and introduce your child to new people, places, and experiences as often as you can. Be adventurous—look at life through your child's eyes as she begins to unearth some of the many wonders of this amazing world in which we live.

Surviving Your Toddler is intended to help you enjoy the toddler years with your child. The ideas contained in this book will help you entertain and stimulate your child through the toddler years while being simple and straightforward enough for even the busiest of parents or caregivers to manage. This book contains suggestions for many situations and occasions, for indoors and outdoors, for summer and winter, for quiet times and active times. While I've written this book as a resource for parents at home with their toddlers, it is well-suited for anyone who has a toddler in their life: mothers or fathers, grandparents, aunts or uncles, babysitters, day-care workers, preschool teachers, church workers, or playgroup leaders. If you spend any time at all with a toddler, then this book is for you.

While many of the ideas in *Surviving Your Toddler* may continue to entertain your child long after the toddler stage, these activities are most suitable for children between the ages of one and three. Because abilities of children in that age range vary greatly, some ideas will be too advanced for a one-year-old, while others will be much too simple for an older three-year-old. Use your judgement in choosing activities that best meet the capabilities and interests of your child. If a new activity doesn't go over quite as well as you expected, don't write it off altogether—try it again in a week, a month, or a year, or vary the activity in a way that will make it more meaningful and interesting for your child.

A note on the use of "his" and "her"; in recognition of the fact that children do indeed come in both genders, and in an effort to represent each, the use of the male and female pronouns will alternate with each chapter.

As my oldest child, my very first baby, approaches adolescence, it has been a special joy to experience the toddler years again. Having several children halfway to adulthood has given me an appreciation of the brevity of these very early years of childhood, an appreciation I didn't have ten years ago when my oldest was a toddler. Although back then it seemed as if my babies would never grow up, most of them have, and yours will, too. Diapers will one day be a thing of the past, as will bottles, soothers, a bathtub full of toys, afternoon naps, sticky fingers, wet kisses, and so many other earmarks of toddlerhood.

Each stage of childhood brings with it its own set of challenges as well as its own special rewards. Some days will bring you more joy than you ever thought possible, while on other days you'll feel grateful if you (or your children) make it through in one piece—this doesn't change, no matter how old your children are! My hope is that you will love your child unconditionally, remember your sense of humour, and relish the toddler years, because, like the fingerprints on the wall, they will be gone before you know it.

TRISH KUFFNER

CHAPTER ONE

Help! I Have a Toddler!

A toddler, according to the dictionary, is one who toddles, which means "to walk with short tottering steps ..." Regardless of what the experts or the outsiders say, those tiny steps will plunge you into one of the most exasperating periods of your adult life.   JAIN SHERRARD

TODDLERS MAY BE DESCRIBED IN MANY WAYS—SOME CALL THEM TERRIBLE (as in "terrible two's"); others call them "terrific" (although I suspect those people do not currently have a toddler in their life). Most toddlers fall somewhere in between. They are wonderful little people some days and a trial other days.

Toddlers are at an interesting stage of development. They can get around on their own, but they need constant supervision. They understand most of what they hear but are usually unable to effectively communicate their wants and needs. They want to do everything for themselves, but their skills and abilities are limited. They want to try everything, and most of what they do is motivated by an interest in cause and effect ("Let's see what happens when ...").

Toddlers also have an abundance of energy. As they enter the toddler stage, some will still be having two naps per day, but by the end of toddlerhood, many will not be napping at all. This means that a parent or caregiver must occupy the toddler for many hours each day, often without a break. This can be a challenge for most adults, whether they are encountering life with a toddler for the first time or experiencing toddlerhood for the second, third, or fourth time.

In addition to their abundant energy and their desire to learn about the world around them, toddlers also have specific needs and characteristics unique to their stage of development. They are not walking babies or watered-down preschoolers. Expecting them to stay involved in activities that are not sufficiently stimulating or too advanced for their abilities will lead to frustration for the child and the parent or caregiver.

What, then, do toddlers need? What activities can a parent or caregiver easily provide that will keep him happy, occupied, and stimulated? Parenting an infant is one thing, but coping with the specific needs of a toddler is something many of us find extremely challenging. Parents at home all day—every day—with a toddler often entertain the thought that "professionals" (early childhood educators or trained and experienced day-care workers) could do a better job of occupying and stimulating their child.

Would your child be happier, better occupied, and more stimulated if he were cared for by professionals? In certain extreme situations, the answer may be yes, but generally most parents lack only experience and confidence. Whether they know it or not, parents usually have enough of what it takes to keep their toddler happy and stimulated. Keep in mind that most of the activities in preschools and day-care centres imitate what can naturally occur in the home on a day-to-day basis: talking, singing, reading, exploring, having a snack, playing outdoors, playing with friends or siblings, napping, and so on. Some may feel that the group setting of a preschool or day-care centre will benefit their child, but toddlers do not learn well, if at all, in group situations. Cynthia Catlin, in her book *Toddlers Together: The Complete Planning Guide for a Toddler Curriculum* (Gryphon House, Beltsville, MD, 1994), says, "Toddlers learn best through their independent explorations and interactions with their caregivers, who can promote their learning by initiating activities based on the children's play behaviours and interest."

This means parents and caregivers are instinctively doing things that stimulate their children to learn. Talking on a toy telephone, asking "Where are your ears?" as you change him, playing hide-and-seek or peek-a-boo, letting him bang about with pots and pans in the kitchen—these activities you've done countless times without thinking you're providing a rich learning environment. You are. Running, sliding, swinging, and playing outside are activities which encourage physical development. Playing with playdough, paints, and crayons develops small muscle skill and promotes creativity. Washing hands before meals teaches health. "Hot! Don't touch!" teaches safety, and a short play-time with friends helps your child learn social skills.

Simply put, toddlers need a stimulating environment and a variety of experiences to help them develop. Activities which emphasize the senses and physical activity will be the most successful. A consistent daily schedule will help your child know what to expect and help him become more independent. He will enjoy repetition of the familiar in songs, books, arts and crafts, and simple games, and he will also be interested in anything new. Try to make a short walk or some outdoor play a part of every day. Be sure to allow your child plenty of free time with interesting things to discover and explore. We all learn best when our interest motivates us to find out about something, and toddlers are no exception.

Don't rely exclusively on books like this when coming up with fun ideas for your toddler. Many ideas that work for others will not work for your child, or they may not work right now. Watch your child, see what types of things interest him, and go from there. Develop your own file or notebook of activities which interest your child. Some may be variations of existing activities, while others will be entirely new. Children under the age of three master skills through repetition—if something works for you, do it over and over and over again. If your child shows no interest in an activity, stop for a time and try it again in a week, month, or year.

ORGANIZING FOR A TODDLER

In many cases, toddlers know how to create their own fun when given the proper materials. Although they require constant supervision, there are things you can do and materials you can provide that will encourage creative and independent play. In all cases, be sure your home is properly "toddler-proofed" with regards to safety. Many small items interesting to toddlers, such as coins and beads, pose an extreme choking hazard. Make sure these items are well out of reach—an especially difficult task if you have older children in the house.

The following suggestions will help you better organize your home to meet your toddler's changing needs. If you have read *Surviving Your Preschooler,* you may recognize some of these ideas (modified for toddlers, of course).

Keep a Baker's Box in the kitchen

Dealing with kitchen tasks can be extremely difficult when combined with keeping an eye on an energetic toddler. At times, one-year-olds may be happy just to sit in their highchair or at their own little table with a few toys or snacks to keep them occupied while you work. At other times, they will want to be right there with you, underfoot and into everything. Kitchen cupboards and drawers are full of interesting things that may prove irresistible to your child.

Why not provide your child with his very own Baker's Box? Put together a collection of unbreakable kitchen tools in a plastic crate or small storage box. Store it in a spare cupboard that is low enough for your child to reach. He can use his tools for play or for helping you do some "real" cooking or baking. Some suggestions for a Baker's Box are

- ▲ cake pan
- ▼ cake rack
- ▶ cookie cutters
- ◀ cookie sheet
- ▼ large metal or plastic bowl
- ▶ measuring spoons
- ◀ muffin tin
- ▼ pie plate
- ▲ plastic measuring cups
- ▼ rubber spatula
- ▶ wooden spoon

Have a Busy Box handy

Since much of our time at home is spent in the kitchen, a spare kitchen cupboard low enough for your child to reach is an ideal spot for his very own Busy Box—a small storage box or plastic crate containing things he can do on his own anytime. An older toddler or preschooler will appreciate many craft-type items in his Busy Box: crayons, markers, colouring books, paper, tape, stickers, scissors, glue, inkpad and rubber stamps, playdough, and so on. But filling a Busy Box for a younger toddler is more of a challenge. Most of us don't want our one-year-old into the tape and markers without close supervision!

Items for a toddler Busy Box must be safe enough for him to play with relatively unsupervised, and they should be things which will not make a mess (at least not much of a mess). Watch what types of things interest your toddler and include those in the Busy Box. For example, if he loves playing with plastic bottles and lids, put some in the box (be sure the lids are big enough to pass the choke test). Most toddlers love to build, so add an assortment of stackable things. Items that work well are empty cereal boxes, thread spools, covered yogourt containers, and individually-wrapped rolls of toilet paper.

Many ideas in this book will help you come up with items suitable for your toddler's Busy Box. In Chapter 2 you will find Sticky Figures, Texture Touch, Surprise Tins, Shaker Bottle, Who Do You See?, Mail Box, Wave Bottle, Bubble Bottle, Clothespin Drop, Clothespin Poke, Grocery Store, What's in the Jar?, Fun with Kleenex, and Squishy Bags.

While most children have favourite things they like to play with, something new to explore and discover will hold their attention and keep them occupied. If you vary the contents of the Busy Box from day to day, your toddler will always find something fresh and exciting to keep him busy and happy.

Set up a Tickle Trunk

A Tickle Trunk full of dress-up clothes and props will not only foster your child's imaginative play but will keep him occupied with all the wonders it contains. Fill a trunk, toybox, large plastic container, or cardboard box with adult clothes, shoes, hats, scarves, gloves, and costume jewelry to use for dress-up. Old suits are great, as are Hawaiian shirts, vests, baseball hats, bridesmaid dresses, nightgowns, wigs, boots, slippers, and purses. Great items can be found at garage sales or local thrift shops, or stock up on princess gowns and animal costumes at post-Halloween sales.

Toddlers may have trouble with zippers and small buttons, so consider replacing the zippers or buttons with velcro, or enlarge the button holes and replace small buttons with large ones that are easy for little fingers to grasp.

Investing in a Tickle Trunk full of dress-up clothes may well be one of the best toys you can assemble for your toddler. Not only will it help keep your child busy and happy in his early years, but chances are it will become an invaluable part of his play for many years to come.

Make up a Rainy Day Box

Although all days with babies, toddlers, and preschoolers can seem long, rainy days seem to have extra hours to fill. When the weather is bad, or when your child is sick, a Rainy Day Box full of surprises can help break the monotony. Good things to put in your Rainy Day Box are:

▲ Fresh, new art supplies (a new pad, markers, paintbox, stickers, or playdough).

◀ A new toy (or one that hasn't been played with in awhile).

▶ A new book, music tape, or video.

◀ Special dress-up items.

▼ Cookie cutters and a new or favourite cookie recipe.

▶ Supplies and directions for a new game or craft (preassemble all supplies and store them in a Ziploc bag in the Rainy Day Box until ready to use).

Don't overuse your Rainy Day Box—it will be regarded with interest and awe only if its appearance is somewhat extraordinary. Store your Rainy Day Box in a safe place and bring it out only when the day seems unusually long.

Make a Job Jar for your child

Whether you're working a full-time job or remain home with your child, whether you're a day-care provider or an occasional babysitter, there will be times when chores need to be done with your toddler close by. Instilling a sense of responsibility toward household chores is something that can be started at this tender age (even very young toddlers like to feel they're helping).

You can make a job jar for your child out of an empty jar, coffee can, or small box. Cut strips of paper and print a small job that needs to be done on each one. Very young toddlers will enjoy wiping the floor or refrigerator with a damp cloth or sponge, stacking towels in a cupboard, or picking up toys and placing them in a basket or container. You will know the jobs your child is capable of doing with minimum supervision and assistance.

Rotate your child's toys

In the first few years of life, most children receive many wonderful toys as gifts for birthdays, Christmas, or other occasions. While parents appreciate the good intentions of the givers, most children have more toys than they can possibly play with. Also, even the most creative toys will fail to hold your child's interest if they're always around. When rotated every four to six weeks, toys will seem new to him and will be interesting and exciting all over again.

Separate your child's toys into piles (if your child has a favourite toy, keep it out all the time). Keep one pile in your child's play area and pack the others away in boxes, marking dates for when they are to be brought out. If you have friends with children the same age, why not try a toy exchange? Keep a list of what's been exchanged and be sure to agree on the terms beforehand (how long, who's responsible for breakage, and so on).

Make a Crazy Can

Someone once referred to the dinner hour as "arsenic hour." Once you've had a toddler or two hanging around at that time, you'll know why! This is usually the time when you are at your busiest and they are at their crankiest. In the midst of the chaos, you yearn for a distraction to keep them busy. It's not a great time to brainstorm for creative activities, so plan ahead with a Crazy Can full of ideas for your toddler.

Make a list of on-the-spot activities that require no special materials, no time-consuming preparation or cleanup, and no serious adult participation or supervision. Write these ideas down on index cards or small pieces of paper and put them in an empty coffee can. If you like, cover the can with cheerful contact paper, or cover it with plain paper and have your child decorate it with paints, markers, or crayons. When things start to get crazy (or when there's just nothing to do), choose a card from the can for an instant remedy. Appendix B at the back of this book offers a list of activities appropriate for a toddler Crazy Can.

Take along a Busy Bag

A Busy Bag will help you be prepared for those times when you just have to wait—at the doctor's office, hairdresser's, restaurant, and so on. Turn a drawstring bag or backpack into a take-along Busy Bag that can be filled with special goodies to keep your child amused. Borrow the portable items from your Busy Box or take along items such as:

- ▲ Dolls and their associated clothing, blankets, bottles, and accessories.
- ◀ An edible necklace (cereal or crackers with holes in the middle strung on a piece of shoestring licorice).
- ▶ A favourite toy, stuffed animal, or blanket.
- ◀ Magnets and a small metal cake pan.
- ▼ Matchbox cars.
- ▲ Simple wooden puzzles.
- ◀ Special snacks.
- ▼ Stickers and a sticker book or plain notebook.

Use your imagination when filling the Busy Bag. You can assemble it yourself so the contents will be a surprise for your child, or you can have your child help you fill the bag before you go. Chapter 6 contains many ideas that will help keep your toddler happy and busy when you're out and about.

Look for new activities and experiences

While children need free time for creative play and unstructured time in which to explore and discover the world around them, they also rely on you to introduce them to new projects, activities, and adventures. This is sometimes hard to do on the spur of the moment, so planning ahead is a good idea. Try to schedule one or two fun, challenging, creative activities each day (not necessarily major projects—sometimes a five-minute game will do). Decide on the activities ahead of time and have all the necessary supplies assembled in advance.

PLANNING YOUR ACTIVITIES

As I mentioned in *Surviving Your Preschooler*, failing to plan is planning to fail. That applies to the big stuff (like saving for your child's education) as well as the little stuff (like a new art project or playing a game with your child). Preschools and day-care centres plan their curriculum carefully to ensure that children have a variety of experiences each day. Parents at home can be somewhat less structured, but the importance of planning new and creative activities should not be overlooked. Children's activity books and resources abound, and can be easily purchased or borrowed from the local library. However, the ideas in these books are only valuable if you use them. If you don't do a little planning, chances are you won't use them. Here are some helpful guidelines for planning your activities:

1. Read this book from cover to cover and create a weekly planner with activities you'd like to try each day. Include a few alternate activities for bad weather days or when things just won't work for what you've planned.

2. Use your weekly activity plan to make a list of supplies you'll need, and assemble or purchase them beforehand.

3. Make a list of what you need to prepare before your child becomes involved in the activity—mix paint, assemble supplies for a game, and so on.

4. Plan special activities for your babysitter, and have all the necessary materials handy. This will let your sitter know that watching TV all day is not an option.

5. Make a list of ideas that would be fun to do anytime you can fit them into your schedule. Have this list ready when you have some unexpected free time.

STOCKING YOUR CRAFT CUPBOARD

Most of the activities in this book require some basic supplies. Whether you use an actual cupboard or just a box in the basement, here are some of the items you'll need to stock your craft cupboard.

Things to save:

aluminum foil • aluminum pie plates (various sizes) • balls (golf, Ping-Pong, tennis) • berry baskets • bottle caps • boxes • bubble wrap • buttons • candles • canning rings • cardboard • catalogues • cereal and pasta bits • cereal boxes • chopsticks • clean, empty food cans • coffee cans with lids • coffee filters • coins • confetti • containers with handles • corks • cotton balls • cotton batting • cotton swabs • diaper-wipe containers • dried beans • dried pasta (different shapes and sizes) •

dried-up markers • egg cartons • egg shells • envelopes • fabric scraps • feathers • felt • film canisters • greeting cards (used) • jars and lids (empty) • junk mail • large, light objects to lift and carry • lids of all kinds • magazines • metal cookie tins • metal lids from frozen juice cans • milk cartons (all sizes) • newspapers • old calendars • old clothes and costume jewelry for dress-up • old magazines • old mittens, socks, gloves for puppets • old sheets • old telephone books • old toothbrushes • paint sample chips • paper bags (all sizes) • paper clips • paper muffin cup liners • paper plates/cups/bowls • paper scraps • paper towel/toilet paper tubes • photographs of friends and family • pine cones • plastic bowls, lids, bottles • plastic milk jugs • plastic yogourt and margarine containers • pop bottles (empty) • popcorn • Popsicle sticks • ribbon scraps • rice (uncooked) • rocks • roll-on deodorant bottles (empty) • rubber bands • salt shakers or spice containers (empty) • sandpaper • scarves (chiffon-type) • shells • shoeboxes with lids • shoelaces • spray bottle • squeeze bottles (the kind mustard and ketchup come in) • stamps • stickers of all kinds • string • Styrofoam trays • swizzle sticks • thread • thread spools • tissue paper scraps • toothpicks • wood scraps • wrapping paper scraps • yarn scraps

Things to buy:

art smock (or use an old shirt) • balloons • beads (large for toddlers) • bells • chalk • child-safe scissors • clear acrylic spray • contact paper (clear and coloured) • clothespins (craft- and spring-type) • coloured cellophane • coloured tape • construction paper in various colours • craft magnets • crayons • crepe paper • elastic • fabric paint • food colouring • glitter • glue gun • glue or glue sticks • googly eyes • hole punch • index cards • liquid starch • magnet strips • masking tape • newsprint pads or rolls • paper clips • paper doilies • paper fasteners • pencil crayons • pencil sharpener • pencils • pens • pipe cleaners • plain writing pads • plastic Easter eggs • plastic tubing • pompoms • rubber cement • ruler • sponges • stapler • stickers • straws • tempera paints and brushes • tissue paper • transparent tape • washable markers • wooden spoons • Ziploc freezer bags

WHAT ABOUT TELEVISION?

The influence of television on children has been much debated over the years. While your child may still be young enough that television is not yet an issue, be assured that it is something you will need to think about carefully in the months and years to come.

As I stated in *Surviving Your Preschooler,* the key to the whole "children and television" issue is not so much what the children watch, because we can control that. I am more concerned about about how parents use television and what children do not do when they watch television. It's easy to use television as a babysitter on occasion, but it can be habit-forming to both parent and child. The few short years of early childhood are better spent playing, reading, walking, talking, painting, and crafting—in other words, doing things together.

But, whether we like it or not, television is here to stay. It's up to parents to use it in a way that will be beneficial to their child's development and their parent/child relationship. How should parents do this?

First, be selective in what your children watch. Good television programs can make learning fun and can expand your child's knowledge of the world. As your toddler gets older, programs like Sesame Street can help him get ready for school. Choose wisely. Look for programs or videotapes which instruct, entertain, and reinforce the values and principles you wish to develop in your child.

Second, limit your child's viewing time each day. Remember, time spent watching TV is time that your child does not spend on other, more valuable activities such as playing games, reading (or being read to), or using his imagination in countless other ways.

Third, watch television with your child whenever possible. Most programs move at a very fast pace in order to hold the attention of their young audience. But young children often have a hard time keeping track of the content, and it is almost impossible for them to stop and ponder what is being presented. By watching with your child, you can provide connections that would otherwise be missed. And by reminding your child of related events in his own life, you help him make sense of what he sees.

Finally, set an example for your child. Show him that you would rather read a book or play a game or talk to him than watch TV. It's hard to expect your child to learn to limit his viewing and choose programs wisely when you do just the opposite. Remember, children learn from our actions more than our words.

A WORD OF ENCOURAGEMENT

Raising a child is a monumental task which brings countless rewards, most of which will be realized only after many years of hard work. But there are also many "warm fuzzies" you receive daily as a parent: the first time your baby smiles at you, his first word, his first step, his warm hugs, and that irresistably cute thing he did that you can't wait to tell Grandma and Grandpa about. As your child moves through the various stages of early childhood, from infant to toddler to preschooler, you will also see the changes that parenting is bringing about in you. You will stretch and grow as a person, you will learn new things (many of them about yourself), and you will develop more patience than you ever thought possible.

If you are parenting a preschooler and a toddler, or a toddler and an infant, or all three (or more) at the same time, the daily challenges you face are even greater. You may not be able to get out as much as you want, or do as many fun and interesting things one-on-one with each child as you'd like, but chances are, if you care enough to read a book such as this, you're already doing a great job. Treasure what you've been given, keep a positive outlook on life, and do the best job you can each day. (They will grow up—I promise!)

Is there only one way to raise happy, healthy, confident, and capable children? Of course not. But by providing your child with daily activities that are simple and fun, by placing more importance on your child's happiness and learning than on the appearance of your home, and by talking to your child on a level he understands, you are well on your way to achieving this goal. Not only will he be better prepared for preschool, kindergarten, and the world beyond, but, in the process, you help to make many happy memories of childhood.

CHAPTER TWO

Rainy Day Play

A Mother's Prayer

Dear Lord,
So far today I've done alright. I haven't gossiped, I haven't lost my temper, I haven't been greedy, grumpy, nasty, selfish, or very indulgent. I'm very grateful for that. But in a few minutes, Lord, I'm going to get out of bed, and from then on, I'm going to need a lot more help.
Amen

MOST PARENTS OF VERY YOUNG CHILDREN WILL AGREE THAT A BOUT OF rainy weather will try the patience of even the calmest, most tolerant among us. Days seem longer, kids seem crankier, and somehow there never seems to be enough to do to keep our energetic little ones occupied.

The west coast of British Columbia where we live is often called "the wet coast." I've had more experience than I'd care to remember dealing with housebound babies, toddlers, and preschoolers. When my three oldest children were young, there were many rainy days when everyone was up at 5 A.M., and our entire day's worth of activities had been completed by about 8 A.M. And there, stretching before us, were at least eight or nine more hours to fill until Daddy came home.

On days like these that seem especially never-ending, my best advice is to get out of the house, if you possibly can. Call a friend and get together for lunch or a midmorning visit. Dress everyone in rain gear and go out for a short walk. If you live close to a fast food restaurant with a "play place", take advantage of it. You don't have to spend a lot. Midmornings and afternoons can be quite slow, and owners don't usually mind you playing for an hour or two if you buy coffee or a juice. You can even go to a mall just to walk around and window shop. We had one close by with a big, indoor fountain, and my little girls spent a fair bit of time throwing pennies into it.

But if you can't get out, for whatever reason, be prepared with lots of fun things for your little ones to do indoors. In many instances, children will create their own fun when given the proper materials:

◀ Put together a collection of things for your toddler to stack. Empty cereal boxes, thread spools, and small yogourt containers with lids work well.

▶ Give your child a variety of safe, unbreakable kitchen objects so she can make her own symphony; wooden spoons, wire whisks, rubber spatulas, pots and pans with lids, and so on.

◀ Place a smooth board against a chair or couch to create a ramp to roll things down.

▼ Help your child create simple puppets out of a paper bag and a cardboard tube.

Don't forget to look in other chapters for more great ideas for indoor fun. Kids in the Kitchen (Chapter 3), Early Learning Fun (Chapter 8), Music and Movement (Chapter 9), and of course Arts and Crafts (Chapter 10) offer countless activities to keep your toddler entertained. While the ideas in this chapter may come in especially handy on rainy days, most are suitable for every day! Many can be easily adapted for outdoor play when the weather is fair.

Inside/Outside Voice

Children are never too young to begin learning consideration of others. Even very young children can be taught this simple rule, and it's a lifesaver on rainy, indoor days.

Ask your child "How many eyes do I have?" "How many ears do I have?" "How many hands do I have?" Go on to explain that we all have two voices, too. One is a great, big, loud voice; the other is a smaller, softer, voice. One voice is good for outside, and one voice is good for inside. Ask her, "Which voice would be good for inside?" and "Which voice are we using now?"

Tape City

Before taping your floor or carpet, test the tape on a small area to be sure it can be easily removed. Leaving the tape on the floor for more than a day may also make it gummy and difficult to remove.

Masking tape
Small cars

Use masking tape on your floor or carpet to create an indoor roadway for small cars. Very young children will enjoy a simple roadway to run their cars along. Older children may enjoy adding parking lots, shops, and schools, and accessorizing with doll houses, toy people, and plastic animals.

Doll Bed

Large cardboard box
Towels or old receiving blankets
Old baby blanket
Small pillow

Make a bed for your child's doll out of a large cardboard box. Use towels or old receiving blankets for bedding. Add a small pillow and a baby blanket if you have one. Your toddler will enjoy putting her baby to bed and waking her up again.

Sheet Day

"Sheet Day" can become an informal holiday in your house every time you strip the beds to change the sheets.

Bed sheets

Since you're stripping the beds anyway, give your child the sheets from all the beds you're changing. She can use them to create houses, tents, forts, or anything else she can dream up. When playtime is over, help your child gather up the sheets and put them in the laundry basket, then take them to the laundry room together.

Unwrapping Game

Small toy
Wrapping paper
Tape

Wrap a small toy in wrapping paper. Show the wrapped toy to your toddler and ask, "What do you think is inside?" Give the wrapped toy to your child so she can remove the paper. Then rewrap the toy as your child watches. Let her unwrap it again and repeat the game until she tires of it.

Texture Touch

Materials of varying textures; sandpaper, old carpeting, fabric, cotton balls, fun fur, and so on
Metal lids from frozen juice cans
Glue
Magnets

Cut the various materials you have gathered into a round shape that will fit the frozen juice can lids. Glue the material onto the lid. Younger toddlers will enjoy simply feeling the textures. Magnets glued to the back of the juice lids will allow your child to play with these on the refrigerator or on a cookie sheet placed on the tray of her highchair.

For older children, make two sets and have them sort the lids by matching the materials or sorting by texture (smoothest to roughest, softest to hardest, and so on).

Sticky Figures

> Flat piece of wood
> Glue gun
> Velcro
> Small figures of animals, dinosaurs, cowboys, and so on

Glue velcro onto a flat piece of wood (try wood of a size that will fit onto the tray of your child's highchair). Glue pieces of velcro onto the bottom of small figures that your child likes to play with. She may amuse herself for quite a while sticking and unsticking these figures on the piece of wood. This technique could also help older children avoid frustration when scenes they are trying to set up keep falling over.

Shaker Bottle

> Clean, empty 500-ml or 1-litre (16- or 32-oz.) pop bottle with cap
> Coloured rice or pasta
> Glue gun or quick bonding glue

Make sure the pop bottle you are using is clean and dry. Place coloured rice or pasta (see Appendix A for instructions on how to dye pasta and rice) into the bottle and glue the cap on. Little ones will love to see what's happening inside as they shake and rattle their bottle.

Surprise Tins

Stack up a few of these in the cupboards that your child explores. She will enjoy discovering what's inside.

> Round, metal cookie tins with lids (or small shoeboxes with lids, or empty diaper-wipe containers)
> Variety of objects: plastic magnetic letters, baby food jar lids, plastic milk bottle caps, small blocks, and so on

Fill several round, metal cookie tins with different objects. Fill one tin with plastic milk bottle caps, another with metal baby food jar lids, a third with small wooden blocks, and so on. Stack these up in a cupboard your child can explore. She will enjoy taking them out, shaking them, taking the lid off (maybe with your help), and discovering what's inside. You can also store things such as the Texture Touch or Picture Sort games in tins or boxes like this.

Ice Cube Bags

> Ice cube tray
> Water
> Red, yellow, and blue food colouring
> Three Ziploc bags

Mix water and food colouring (enough for two ice cubes of each colour) and pour into an ice cube tray. When frozen, place a red and a yellow ice cube into one Ziploc bag, a red and a blue ice cube into the second Ziploc bag, and a yellow and a blue ice cube into the third Ziploc bag. Younger children will enjoy moving the ice cubes around in the bags, while older children will enjoy watching what happens when the two colours melt together.

Bottles and Lids

> Collection of bottles and lids of varying sizes

Save small plastic bottles with screw-type lids. Your toddler will have lots of fun matching lids to bottles, putting the lids on, taking the lids off, and starting all over again. A bottle collection is also great fun for the bath, or for water play outdoors.

Flashlight Fun

Flashlight

Shine a flashlight on different parts of a room: the wall, the door, the floor, and so on. Each time you shine the light on an object, name it: for example, "This is the bed." Show your child how to turn the flashlight on and off. Let her shine it on various objects and name them. Give her directions to follow, such as "Shine the light on the ceiling."

Who Do You See?

Small mirror
Box with lid
Glue
Colourful contact paper, construction paper, or giftwrap (optional)

Glue a small mirror inside a box. If you like, decorate the outside of the box and lid with colourful contact paper, construction paper, or giftwrap. Place the lid on top of the box. When your child opens the box, she will see someone special!

If you don't have a small mirror (or don't want your child playing with something breakable), glue photographs or other pictures to the inside of the box. Use photos of your child, her friends, her family, or pictures of people, animals, or other objects cut from magazines or greeting cards.

Fun with Tape

Simple as it may seem, a small piece of tape can provide young children with a lot of enjoyment. Collect a few different kinds of colourful plastic tape, masking tape, double-sided tape, and so on. Your toddler will sometimes enjoy using tape in place of glue when making a collage.

Pieces of tape

Give your young child one or two pieces of tape to play with. She may try sticking them together, to herself, to you, or to other objects around the house. Be sure to watch her if you're worried about the tape sticking to precious books or papers that may be in her path.

Highchair Fun

Be sure to use string that is not long enough to pose a choking hazard, and never leave your child unattended in her highchair.

Short lengths of string
Small toys
Tape (optional)

Tie one end of short lengths of string to a few of your child's toys. Tie or tape the other ends to the tray of her highchair. She will enjoy throwing the toys off the highchair tray, then pulling the strings to get them back again.

Porcupine Playdough

Playdough
Wooden Popsicle sticks or plastic drinking straws

Give your child a lump of playdough and a bunch of wooden Popsicle sticks or plastic drinking straws. Show her how to poke the sticks or straws into the playdough to make a porcupine.

Simple Sorter

If you don't have any Ping-Pong or golf balls handy, try using round plastic milk jug lids instead.

> Ping-Pong or golf balls
> Plastic container with lid

Cut a hole big enough for a Ping-Pong or golf ball to fit through in the lid of the plastic container. Place the lid on the container and let your toddler have fun poking the balls through the hole. She will quickly learn how to remove the lid to retrieve the balls, but will need your help to replace the lid on the container so she can start over again.

Block Sorter

> Shoebox with lid
> Wooden blocks (square, cylinder and rectangle)
> Marker
> Scissors

Place the blocks on the shoebox lid and trace around them. Cut around the outline of each shape. Place the lid on the shoebox and give the blocks to your toddler. She will have lots of fun poking the shapes through the holes, opening the lid, retrieving the shapes, and starting over again.

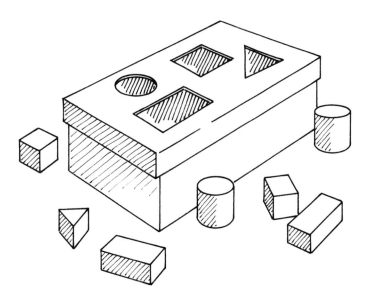

Threading

Shoe lace or thin plastic tubing

Items for threading: empty thread spools, large beads, hair curlers, large pasta, paper towel tubes cut into one-inch rings

Collect a variety of circular objects such as empty spools, large beads, plastic hair curlers, large pieces of pasta, or paper towel tubes cut into one-inch rings. Show your child how to thread these items onto a shoe lace or length of thin plastic tubing. Tie one of the objects being threaded to the end of the lace or tubing to prevent the rest from slipping off as they are threaded.

Ring Fun

Small plastic container
Playdough
Wooden spoon
Canning rings

Fill a small plastic container with playdough and insert a wooden spoon in the middle. (If you want to keep your child's fingers out of the playdough, use a container with a lid; cut a hole in the lid big enough for the wooden spoon to go through.) Give your child a stack of canning rings and show her how to place the rings over the end of the wooden spoon.

Mail Box

Shoebox with lid
Scissors
Unopened junk mail

Cut a large slit in the lid of a shoebox. If you like, cover the box and lid (separately) with coloured paper, or decorate with paints, markers, and stickers. Place the lid on the box and show your toddler how to "mail" letters. Store the mail inside the box when play is over.

Bubble Bottle

Clean, empty 500-ml or 1-litre (16- or 32-oz.) pop bottle with cap
Water
Tempera paint
Liquid detergent

Fill the clean pop bottle with water to about one-third full. Add a spoon or two of tempera paint and about one-third of a cup of liquid detergent. Glue the cap securely onto the bottle by applying glue to the inside of the bottle cap and screwing it on. Your child will enjoy shaking the bottle to make coloured bubbles.

Wave Bottle

Clean, empty 500-ml or 1-litre (16- or 32-oz.) pop bottle with cap
Water
Food colouring
Glitter, sequins, or beads (optional)
Baby oil
Glue gun or quick bonding glue

Fill the clean pop bottle with water to about one-third full. Add a few drops of food colouring and glitter, sequins, or beads (optional), then fill the rest of the bottle with baby oil. Glue the cap securely onto the bottle by applying the glue to the inside of the bottle cap and screwing it on. Your child will enjoy gently shaking the bottle back and forth to produce beautiful waves.

Clothespin Drop

Clean, plastic 2- or 4-litre (one-half or one gallon) milk jug with lid
Clothespins (about 6 or 8)

Put the clothespins in the jug and screw on the lid. Your toddler will enjoy shaking the jug with the clothespins inside. Show her how to remove the lid (or do it for her if she can't quite do it on her own), shake the clothespins out, then one-by-one drop them back in again.

For variety, use a couple of spoons in place of clothespins. They make an interesting sound when the jug is shaken.

Clothespin Poke

Empty egg carton
Clothespins

Turn the egg carton upside down and punch small holes (just big enough to fit the clothespin) in the bottom of each section. Place clothespins in the holes and let your toddler have fun taking them out and putting them back in again.

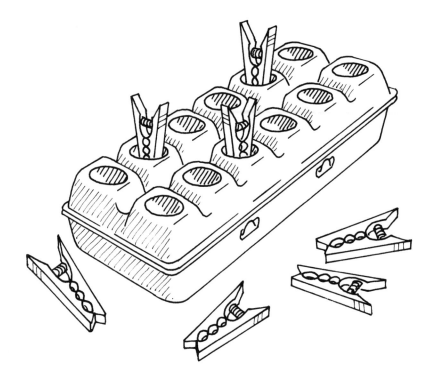

Clothespin Can

> Craft-type clothespins (without a spring)
> Empty coffee can

Show your toddler how to place the clothespins around the rim of the coffee can. You can also cut a small hole in the plastic lid of the can and have her drop the clothespins through the hole. She'll like the sound they make as they hit the bottom. Store the clothespins in the covered coffee can when not in use.

Rock Play

Johanna, my toddler-in-residence while I was writing this book, loved to play with rocks. No matter where we were outside, she was sure to be found playing with rocks. Of course rocks found their way inside, and we found them everywhere: with her toys, in her crib, in the bathtub, and inside cupboards. She never seemed to tire of her little rock collection.

> Rocks
> Containers
> Basket with handle

Take your toddler on a walk outside. Bring along a plastic bucket or basket with handle and collect rocks as you walk. Be sure to choose rocks big enough to pass the choke test (or simply discard the smaller ones when you return home). When you get home, wash them off and set them out with some containers for your child to play with. She will enjoy placing them one-by-one in the containers, dumping them out, carrying them around with her in a basket, and putting them in her pockets or purse. She may also enjoy painting them or placing them in a covered coffee can to make a loud shaker toy.

Nuts and Bolts

> Large nuts and bolts

Purchase several large bolts and a lot of nuts and keep them on hand for your older child (probably three and up). She will enjoy screwing nuts on and off the bolts, and you can use this as a counting activity, too.

Indoor Sandbox

In *Surviving Your Preschooler,* I suggest making an indoor sandbox by filling up a cardboard box or plastic baby bath with puffed wheat or rice cereal or uncooked rice. Here are some alternatives that may be purchased fairly inexpensively in bulk and provide an interesting sensory experience for toddlers. If you're concerned about your child eating the material, please supervise closely.

> water softener salt
> birdseed
> dried beans
> oatmeal
> cornmeal
> shredded paper
> cedar shavings
> deer corn
> foam packing peanuts
> potting soil (if you're brave!)

Children enjoy playing in the sandbox with cups, spoons, bowls, buckets, scoops, shovels, cars, and other toys and containers. A funnel and scoop that can be used to fill an empty plastic pop bottle with sandbox material will also be a hit. An old sheet, shower curtain, or plastic tablecloth placed under the sandbox makes cleanup a little easier.

All Gone!

> Two large containers
> Basket or small bucket with handle
> Small toys

Fill one large container with small toys. Place the empty container across the room or some distance away from the full one. Show your child how to fill her basket with toys from the full container, carry them across the room, and dump them into the empty container. It may take more than one trip to empty the first container, or she may decide to take them back to the first container right away. Whenever a container is empty, say "All gone!"

Grocery Store

Toddlers have fun filling up bags and baskets with just about anything. For variety, use blocks or Duplo in place of the groceries suggested here.

> Paper bag with handles or small basket
> Empty food boxes and containers
> Glue gun

Save up empty food boxes and containers. Pudding or jelly powder boxes work well, as do cereal boxes, small yogourt containers, and empty vitamin bottles. Seal the boxes with tape. Use a glue gun to permanently attach the lids to the small containers. (They may be a choking hazard.) Store all your "groceries" in a box or laundry basket. Your child will have fun "going shopping" with a paper bag or small basket.

Sticky Feet

> Clear contact paper
> Tape

Cut a piece of clear contact paper at least two feet long. Remove the backing and tape the contact paper, sticky side up, to the floor or carpeting. Toddlers will have fun running, jumping, dancing, or just standing on the paper. Not only will their feet stick to the paper, but lifting them makes a wonderful sound.

What's In the Jar?

Toddlers always love taking lids off small containers and jars. How much more fun when there's an interesting toy inside!

> Small clear plastic jars with lids
> Small toys that will fit into each jar

Place a small, colourful toy into a clear plastic jar and close the lid. Give your toddler the jar and let her remove the lid and retrieve the toy inside. She'll probably want to do it again and again.

Bear in the Basket

What parent hasn't come into their child's room after naptime and discovered every doll, bear, animal, and blanket from the crib all over the floor? Children won't need much help catching on to this game!

> Stuffed animals
> Large basket or container

Place a large basket or container next to your child's crib (empty laundry baskets or hampers work well). Place her in the crib along with a teddy bear or supply of stuffed animals or other soft, light toys. Show her how to drop the bear into the basket. You may want to count to her, "One, two, three, drop the bear!"

Pull Box

> Small box without lid
> Thick rope

Punch a small hole in one end of the small box (a shoebox is ideal). Insert one end of the rope through the hole and tie a knot so that the rope will not pull through the hole. Your child will have fun filling her box with blocks, rocks, small toys, or other objects and pulling it behind her around the room or outside on a walk.

Nesting Cans

I bought a popular set of twelve nesting cups when my first child was an infant. Ten years later, I don't think anyone (other than myself) has ever put all twelve cups back in order! Three or four cups or cans are sufficient for most toddlers.

> Three or four cans that will fit inside each other
> Duct tape
> Scissors
> Contact paper or construction paper

Make a set of nesting cans by saving three or four cans that fit inside each other. Make sure there are no sharp inside edges, then cover the rim of each can with duct tape. Cover each can with contact paper or construction paper. Your child will have fun dumping the cans then fitting them back together. Turn the cans upside down to build a tower.

For a sorting activity, make two or three sets of nesting cans. Cover each set in a different colour or pattern of contact or construction paper.

Where's Teddy?

> Teddy bear or plush toy
> Long string

Tie one end of a long string around one of your child's plush toys or her favourite teddy bear. Hide the bear under a bed or in a closet or drawer. Trail the string from the bear's hiding place around the room, over and under furniture, out the door, down the hall, as far as you like. Give the end of the string to your child and say, "Where's Teddy?" (or the toy's name). Help her follow the string to find the bear.

Chair Maze

> Chairs

This activity will work outdoors as well as in. Place chairs in a maze around the room. Let your child crawl through them or walk over them, or use them as a train for her stuffed animals.

Fun with Kleenex

Most toddlers have probably tried this on their own at one time or another.

> Box of Kleenex

Give your toddler a box of Kleenex and let her pull the Kleenex out one by one. The fun your toddler will have and the time she spends on this will justify the price of the box of Kleenex! If you'd rather not use real Kleenex, stuff a few scarves or pieces of brightly coloured tissue paper into an empty Kleenex box and let your child pull those out instead.

Jungle Safari

This is a great way to get your toddlers and preschoolers to bed at night.

> Stuffed animals
> Flashlight

Just before bedtime, when pyjamas are on and teeth are brushed, hide your child's stuffed animals in odd places around the house (for really young children, you may have to hide them in rather obvious places at first). Turn off the lights and use a flashlight to hunt for the animals hiding in your house.

Monkey, Monkey!

Too often parents focus on the "bad" things children do, while letting the "good" slip by without comment. This is a simple way to reinforce and reward cooperation and kindness.

> Plastic linking monkeys

Place a plastic monkey on the wall in a place where you can add more monkeys to make a chain. When you catch your child being especially kind and cooperative (that is, playing quietly with siblings, helping out without being asked, picking up toys without being reminded, and so on), reward her with a monkey to add to the chain. When the last monkey is hung, treat the whole family to an ice cream sundae, video rental, or special afternoon of games.

Toddler Train

Your child will enjoy filling up each car with her "stuff" and pulling this train behind her wherever she goes.

> Assorted boxes (three or more)
> String, ribbon, or yarn
> Plastic straws
> Scissors

Use scissors or another pointed object to poke small holes in the ends of each box. Insert about a foot of string, ribbon, or yarn into the back hole of the first box, and tie the string around a short piece of plastic straw to prevent it from pulling back out through the hole. Insert the string through the front hole of the next box and fasten it in the same way. Use another length of string for the next box, and continue in this way until the boxes are all connected. Use a longer length of string or ribbon for the front hole of the first box. Tie a cylindrical wooden block or small plastic vitamin bottle to the end of this string as a handle which your child can pull.

Blanket Riding

This activity works best on smooth flooring such as hardwood, linoleum, or ceramic.

> Blanket, sheet, or large towel

Sit your child in the middle of a blanket, sheet, or large towel. Grasp the edge of the blanket and gently pull her around the room.

Cartons of Fun

This idea is recommended for older two- and three-year-olds, as younger children will likely not get any more creative than dumping the contents on the floor.

Empty milk cartons or other containers
Miscellaneous craft items

Fill clean empty milk cartons with an assortment of craft items: scraps of fabric, ribbon, wrapping paper, bows, stickers, glue, safety scissors, and so on. Bring out the carton for a fun and creative playtime.

Napkin Bug

Even much older children will have fun with this one.

Paper towel
Medium-sized orange, grapefruit, or plastic ball
Pen or marker

Place the orange, grapefruit, or plastic ball on a flat surface and put one piece of paper towel over it so that the fruit is roughly centred under the towel. Cup your hand over the paper towel so that it moulds around the fruit (this is the body of the bug). Using your other hand, twist each corner of the paper towel around and around until you have twisted right up to the body (these are the legs). Use a pen or marker to draw a face on the bug, then roll the fruit to make the bug run (the rather jerky roll of the fruit gives the bug a funny little run). If you like, make a couple of bugs and race them against each other.

Potty Pals

I've never used this idea myself, but one mom says it's the one thing that helped get her three-year-old out of diapers.

> Colourful contact paper
> Scissors

Cut out eyes and a happy smile from contact paper and stick them to the bottom of each toilet seat your child will be using. (Don't forget the cover of your child's potty, if she has one.) Your child can name each friend and assume responsibility for visiting and "feeding" them throughout the day. If your child likes this idea, it can make going to the potty an exciting event rather than something she wants to avoid.

Nursing Basket

This is a great idea for the toddler who seems to need something everytime you sit down to nurse or feed your new baby. If you don't have a baby to feed, trying putting together a Telephone Basket for when you need to make a few phone calls without interruptions.

> Small basket, box, drawstring bag, or plastic storage container
> Snacks, special toys, books, and so on

Put together a nursing basket for your toddler by assembling a collection of special snacks, toys, books, or other treats that can be brought out only when you nurse the baby. When you're finished nursing or feeding your baby, put the basket away until the next time.

Cereal Box Puzzles

Colourful cereal boxes make an inexpensive jigsaw puzzle that can be tailored for your child's age and ability.

> Empty cereal boxes
> Scissors

Cut out the front panel of an empty cereal box. Cut into interlocking shapes, making the size of the pieces and the difficulty of the puzzle appropriate for the child who will be putting the puzzle together.

Interrupt Rule

When you're talking on the phone or in person with someone, teach your child how to interrupt politely. Show her how to place her hand on your arm, shoulder, or leg. This will be her signal to you that she needs your attention. Place your hand over hers as your signal that you understand and will acknowledge her as soon as politely possible. Very young children should not be made to wait more than 10 or 15 seconds, but this time can and should grow longer as your child becomes used to this rule.

Mini Mask

Paper
Scissors
Pencil, markers, or crayons
25-cent coin

Cut a small (4- to 6-inch) square of paper. Place the coin in the middle of the square and trace around it. Draw eyes above the circle and a mouth below it. Be creative in adding eyelashes, eyebrows, or a funny moustache. Cut out the circle in the centre of the mask and put it on your child's face by placing the centre hole over her nose.

I Think I Can

For this activity you'll need the book, *The Little Engine That Could,* by Watty Piper. Libraries will have a copy, but this is one of those books you'll want to own.

The Little Engine That Could (book)

Read the story of *The Little Engine That Could* to your child. Talk about how the little engine thought she could make it up the hill, even though it was a very hard thing to do. Ask her if she thinks she can do something that may seem hard at first, then play the "I Think I Can" game. Ask your child to try different things like, "Can you hop on one foot?" or "Can you touch your toes?" Demonstrate for her, then say "I think I can, I think I can" as you hop or bend together. Try this game when you're encouraging your child to pick up her toys ("Do you think you can put away all your cars before I pick up these puzzles?").

People Puppets

Photos of family members
Glue or tape
Clear contact paper
Popsicle sticks

Use glue or tape to attach a Popsicle stick to the back of a photograph. Cover with clear contact paper for an instant puppet.

Easy Bird Feeder

Feeding the birds is fun, but once you start it's important to keep it up for the whole season. Birds will come to rely on the food you provide and may have difficulty finding another food source if you suddenly stop.

Round oat cereal or circular pretzels
Heavy string, yarn, or a shoelace

String round oat cereal or circular pretzels onto heavy string, yarn, or a shoelace. Tie the ends together and hang in a tree to feed the birds.

Flying Fish

Page from an old magazine
Pencil
Ruler
Scissors

Using the ruler, pencil, and scissors, mark and cut a strip of the magazine page that is as long as the page and one inch wide. Mark a line on both ends of the strip that is one inch from end. Cut a slit halfway into the strip at each point (at one end of the strip cut from the top halfway down to the middle, and at the other end cut from the bottom halfway up to the middle). Bend the strip into a loop and push the slits together so that the loop closes. Toss the fish into the air to see it fly.

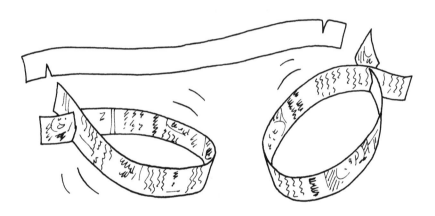

Early Morning Fun

If your toddler is an early riser, you may find this idea will give you a few extra minutes of precious sleep.

Basket or small plastic crate
Two or three quiet toys, games, or activities

Before you go to bed at night, put two or three quiet toys, games, or activities in a basket or small plastic crate. Be sure that the items you choose are completely safe for your child to play with unsupervised. Place the basket or crate in your toddler's crib or beside her bed. The toys or activities may keep her occupied long enough for you to make the coffee, have a shower, or just enjoy a little extra sleep!

Toddler Pouch

Toddlers love to collect things in their pockets. They will enjoy wearing this little pouch and using it to store all their interesting discoveries.

> Two paper plates
> Scissors
> Stapler
> Hole punch
> Yarn or ribbon

Cut one paper plate in half. Staple one half to the second paper plate to form a pouch. Punch two holes in the top of the full paper plate, and tie a short length of yarn or ribbon from one hole to the next to form a handle. (Because of the danger of strangulation, please be sure that the length of yarn or ribbon is not long enough to go over your child's head.) Decorate it with crayons, markers, or stickers. Hang the pouch from your child's belt or let her carry it around with her.

Magic Mud

Magic Mud feels like a solid, but just drips through your fingers.

> One box cornstarch
> Water
> Food colouring

Put the cornstarch in a bowl. Add just enough water to be able to stir it, then add food colouring. Your child may just want to use her fingers to play with this, but it's great for running cars through, too.

Squishy Bag

3½ cups water
4 tablespoons cornstarch
Food colouring
Ziploc bag

Boil the water. In a separate bowl, add cold water to the cornstarch to make a paste. Slowly add the cornstarch mixture to the boiled water. Cook and stir until thick. Add food colouring and allow to cool. Pour into a Ziploc bag and seal. Children can squish the bag without opening it.

No-Cook Squishy Bag

Try the following no-cook alternatives to the Squishy Bag. Make sure the bag is well-sealed before letting your child squish it. You can vary the sensory experience by warming or chilling the contents before giving them to your toddler. You could also use two at a time, one warm and one cold.

hair gel and a few drops of food colouring
ketchup and mustard
shaving cream with or without food colouring
toothpaste
hand lotion
thick fingerpaint
pudding
snow (for a temporary and seasonal activity)

Painting Bag

Although this idea uses paint, I think it's too neat and clean to include with the other painting activities. It's quick and fun for anytime—not just when you've got the time and energy for a painting project.

3 tablespoons powdered tempera paint
¼ cup liquid laundry starch (optional)
Ziploc bag
Construction paper

Mix the powdered tempera paint with liquid laundry starch. Pour it into the bag and smooth out the bubbles. If you don't have liquid laundry starch, just mix the tempera paint fairly thickly, or use fingerpaint. Make sure the bag is well-sealed, then show your child how to press the bag to make designs. Place a piece of construction paper under the bag (use a different colour than the paint) and notice how it seems to change the colour of the paint.

Pipe Play

Your child should have years of fun building structures with these pipes and connectors.

> 10- to 20-foot length of 1-inch PVC pipe
> PVC joints

Cut a 10- to 20-foot length of 1-inch PVC pipe into various lengths ranging from four to ten inches. Add various PVC joints to serve as connectors (these come straight or in a T, L or + shape). Building with these pipes and connectors will keep children of all ages occupied indoors on a rainy day. In fine weather, your child will enjoy building outside. Add a garden hose so she can run water through her pipes.

Tube Fun

A short length of flexible transparent tubing from the hardware store can be used in several ways to provide some simple fun for your toddler.

> 3-foot length of flexible transparent tubing, about 1-inch in diameter
> Marbles
> Cork
> Glue gun

Glue a cork securely in one end of the tube. Put several marbles inside the tube and glue a cork in the other end. Your child will have fun seeing the marbles roll as she lifts the tube by one end or in the middle. For an alternative, use a shorter length of tubing and fill with vegetable oil before adding the marbles (be sure the corks fit very tightly for this one!).

Tubes and Balls

Small balls such as golf balls, Ping-Pong balls, or tennis balls
Cardboard tubes from paper towel or large, giftwrap rolls
Scissors
Box or basket

Collect a variety of small balls that are big enough to avoid a choking hazard. Cut various widths of cardboard tubes into different lengths. Put the balls and tubes in a box or basket and let your child have fun dropping the balls through the tubes.

Net Ball

This makes a big, light ball that's safe and easy for even the youngest child to use indoors or out.

Onion-bag netting
Cotton batting or cotton balls
Twist tie or elastic band

Stuff the onion-bag netting with as much cotton as possible. Knot the top of the bag with a twist tie or elastic band.

Tube Ball

Large cardboard mailing tube or giftwrap tube
Tennis ball
String
Empty basket or box

Tie a large cardboard tube to a stair railing, making the end of the tube even with the end of the railing. Place a basket or box at the end of the tube. Your toddler will enjoy placing the ball in one end and watching it shoot out the other end into the basket. This will keep your little one busy for a long time, especially if she has to climb down the steps to retrieve the ball and back up to play again. If you don't want her climbing the steps on her own, give her a small stool to step on to reach the top end of the tube, or avoid stools and steps altogether by placing one end of the tube on a couch and the other end on the floor.

Balls, Balls, Balls

Children get so much enjoyment from balls. Instead of using a "real" ball, try using rolled up socks, crumpled up newspaper taped into a ball, or make a Net Ball (see page 52). These ideas can be easily adapted for either indoor or outdoor play.

> Soft ball
> Empty box or laundry basket
> Slide or board
> Empty plastic pop bottles

▲ Sit opposite your child with your legs apart and take turns rolling the ball back and forth to each other.

◀ Turn the box or basket on its side and show your child how to roll the ball into the target.

▶ Place an empty box or laundry basket on the floor and have your child toss the ball into the basket from several feet away.

◀ Place the basket on top of a dresser for a game of indoor basketball.

▼ Using a slide or a board propped against a chair or the stairs, show your child how to roll the ball down it. Then try rolling the ball up the slide or board.

▶ Line up three or four empty plastic pop bottles, then roll a large rubber ball and try to knock them over.

Fun with Balls

> Muffin pan
> Tennis, golf, or Ping-Pong balls
> Small basket or plastic container with handle (optional)

Give your toddler several tennis, golf, or Ping-Pong balls (or an assortment of all three) and an empty muffin pan. She will have fun putting the balls in each compartment, dumping them out, collecting them up, and starting all over again. If you like, provide her with a small basket or plastic container into which she can put the balls as she picks them up.

People Blocks

Pictures of family members
Clear contact paper
Rectangular wood blocks or clean, empty food cans

Use clear contact paper to attach photographs of your family to rectangular blocks of wood or clean, empty food cans. Your child will love building structures with her people blocks.

Toddler Blocks

Empty milk cartons (any size will do)
Tape
Colourful contact paper, fabric, construction or wrapping paper

Choose two milk cartons the same size. Measure the base of the carton, and make a cutting line that same distance up the side of the carton. Cut along the lines on both cartons. You should now have two open-ended cubes. Push one cube into the other so that all sides are closed. Tape around the cut edges.

The cubes you make can be covered in any way you like. Use colourful contact paper, construction paper, fabric, or wrapping paper. You can also glue on photos of your child, her friends and family, or pictures cut from magazines. If using construction paper, wrapping paper, photos, or pictures, cover with clear contact paper to make the block more durable.

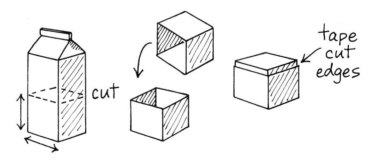

Sponge Blocks

Sponges make ideal blocks for toddlers. They are easy to hold, lightweight, and won't hurt anybody or anything if thrown.

Large, thick sponges

Purchase a colourful variety of large, thick sponges for your toddler to use as blocks. If you like, cut some in halves, quarters, or in triangular or other shapes. Store them in a laundry basket or plastic storage bin. Older toddlers may enjoy sorting sponges by colour or making a pattern with them.

Paper Bag Blocks

Toddlers love to lift and carry these big, light blocks. They're rather hard to store but easy to make again another day.

    Paper grocery bags
    Newspapers
    Packing tape

Lay a paper bag flat on a floor or table. Fold the top over six to eight inches and make a crease. Scrunch up newspaper one sheet at a time and fill the bag to the fold line. Fold the top over and tape the bag closed. If you like, paint or decorate the blocks before using. Make a tunnel for your child to crawl through or a tower for her to knock down, or just let her carry them around the house.

Stacking Fun

    Individually-wrapped toilet paper rolls
    Small cans of tuna, tomato paste, and so on

Look around your house for interesting items for your toddlers to stack. If you buy toilet paper in individually-wrapped rolls, your child will have great fun using them to build towers. Small cans of tuna or tomato paste also stack nicely and are easy for little hands to manage.

Balloon Fun

One or more helium-filled balloons
String or ribbon

Attach a length of string or ribbon to a helium-filled balloon. The string or ribbon should be just long enough so that your child can reach the string when the balloon is resting on the ceiling. Your child will have fun pulling the balloon down, letting it go, and watching it rise back up to the ceiling again. Supervise carefully to avoid the danger of your child choking on a piece of broken balloon.

Balloon Play

Remember, balloon pieces can pose an extreme choking hazard for children, so any balloon play with toddlers must be carefully supervised.

Wooden paint stirrer
Large paper plate
Glue gun
Balloons

Use a hot glue gun to attach a large paper plate to the end of a wooden paint stirrer. Throw the balloon up in the air and ask your toddler to try to catch the balloon in the paper plate, or have fun simply batting the balloon around. Put on some lively music to add to the fun.

More Balloon Fun

Balloons

String

Plastic baseball bat, plastic golf club, giftwrap tube, or rolled up newspaper

Inflate five or six balloons and tie the ends securely. Attach a length of string or ribbon to each balloon. Suspend the bunch of balloons from the ceiling so that they hang just beyond your child's reach. Let your toddler use a plastic baseball bat or golf club to bat at the bunch of balloons. If you don't have a bat or golf club, use a cardboard giftwrap tube, or make a bat by rolling up several sheets of newspaper and taping them securely. Remember to supervise carefully when young children are playing with balloons.

Beanbag Crawl

If making your own beanbag, place the dried beans in a small Ziploc bag before filling the beanbag. The freezer bag protects the beans even if the bag gets wet.

Beanbag

Place a beanbag on your child's back while she's in a crawling position. Have her crawl around the room until the beanbag falls off. Two toddlers will enjoy playing this game, with one crawling and the other picking up the beanbag when it falls. Older children can play with a friend or sibling, seeing who can keep the beanbag on their back the longest.

Beanbag Races

One child can race against the clock, while two or more children can race against either the clock or each other.

Beanbag

Clock (optional)

Decide on a starting line and a finish line. Have children race with a beanbag balanced on their head or squeezed between their knees. Very young children can balance the beanbag in an open palm or kick the beanbag across the finish line.

Hide the Beanbag

Beanbag

Have your child close her eyes while you hide a beanbag within a defined area. When she finds the beanbag, it's her turn to hide it while you close your eyes.

Beanbag Throw

Beanbag
Basket

Throw a beanbag into a basket and ask your child to bring you the beanbag. Repeat as long as this holds her attention. She may want to try throwing the beanbag into the basket herself or may just walk to the basket and drop it in.

Indoor Baseball

Games such as this help your toddler develop eye-body coordination and are suitable for indoor play as well as out.

Empty giftwrap roll
Balloon

Play baseball with an inflated balloon and an empty giftwrap roll. Take turns hitting, throwing, and running bases. Due to the extreme choking hazard posed by pieces of broken balloon, remember to always supervise carefully when young children are playing with balloons.

Toddler Bowling

Empty plastic pop bottles, or unopened paper towel rolls
Large rubber ball

Line up three or four (or more) empty plastic pop bottles or unopened paper towel rolls. Show your toddler how to roll a large rubber ball to knock them over.

Toddler Obstacle Course

An obstacle course is great fun for a group of toddlers at a birthday party, or in a Sunday School class, playgroup, or other group setting. You can also use it at home for your own toddler and/or preschooler.

Come up with fun ideas for an obstacle course for your child or group. Bear in mind the ages, abilities, and number of children who will be involved, as well as the space you have available. Keep it simple to start with, and change the components of the course as your child masters them. Keep in mind that most toddlers will need the help of an older child or adult to make it through the obstacle course, especially the first time.

The following ideas will get you started. Four or five stations are probably enough for a very young group (older preschoolers should be able to manage up to ten).

- ▲ Jump over a rope.
- ◀ Walk along a balance board or a line of tape on the floor.
- ▶ Build a tower with blocks or other stackable objects.
- ◀ Roll a ball into a target or down a slide.
- ▼ Clip clothespins around the rim of a coffee can.
- ▲ String some beads on a shoelace.
- ◀ Draw a picture or scribble on a piece of paper.
- ▼ Play a game of newspaper golf with a rolled-up newspaper and a golf ball.
- ▲ Drop objects into a simple shape sorter.
- ◀ Play a simple matching game (correcly match up two sets of objects).
- ▶ Knock down paper towel rolls or empty pop bottles with a large ball.
- ◀ Thread canning rings on a wooden spoon.
- ▼ Crawl through or walk over chairs placed in a maze around the room.
- ▲ Jump into and out of a Hula-Hoop two or more times.
- ◀ Hammer golf tees into a piece of styrofoam with a toy hammer.
- ▼ Toss a soft ball or rolled up socks into an empty laundry basket.

Mini Olympics

Paper plates and/or straws
Newspaper
Marker

Make a bullseye by drawing a large circle on a sheet of newspaper. Standing back a few feet, have your child try to throw the "discus" (paper plate) so that it lands on the bullseye. Vary this game by using drinking straws as javelins.

Big Mouth Game

Cardboard box
Markers
Scissors
Newspaper or tissue paper for decorating
Glue
Tennis balls, or rolled-up pairs of socks

Draw a happy face on the side of a closed cardboard box. Make sure to draw a big, smiling, open mouth. Cut out the mouth. Add hair to the top of the box by gluing strips of newspaper or tissue paper so they hang down the sides. Stand back a suitable distance and see how many balls can be thrown into the mouth.

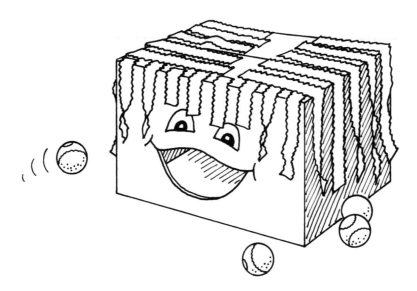

Musical Animals

This is an easier and more suitable (for younger children) version of the familiar musical chairs game.

    Stuffed animals, one for each player
    Chairs, one for each player (optional)
    Music

Place several chairs in a circle and put a stuffed animal on each chair, or place the animals in a circle on the floor. Toddlers walk around the circle and, when the music stops, each player picks up an animal and sits down. Players then take turns acting out that animal. If you don't have enough stuffed animals, paste pictures of various animals on sheets of paper and tape them to the chairs or place them in a circle on the floor.

If only you and your child are playing this game, place the stuffed animals inside a pillowcase. Take turns removing an animal from the pillowcase and acting it out.

CHAPTER THREE

Kids in the Kitchen

Children are natural mimics—they act like their parents in spite of every attempt to teach them good manners.

ANONYMOUS

SEVERAL TIMES THROUGHOUT THIS BOOK YOU WILL READ THAT FOR TODdlers it's the process, not the product, that counts. The value of an activity comes from what they do and what they learn, rather than what they produce. That's certainly worth remembering for most activities, such as art and crafts, but in the kitchen it's a little different story. In the kitchen the product does count! Kids may have fun dumping in a whole box of salt, and they may learn that salt comes quickly from the box when you turn it upside down, but unfortunately you will end up with an inedible product and a disappointed child!

One-year-olds will often be happy just to sit in their highchair or at their own table with a small container of cereal or raisins to occupy them while you work. An empty egg carton to put their little snacks in will often keep them busy for a long time. But if they insist on helping, there are lots of ways to accommodate them without putting your delicious food in danger:

▲ Bake cupcakes and mix frosting ahead of time, and let your toddler ice them with a small plastic knife or Popsicle stick.

▼ When making cookies, roll a bit of dough into a log and let your child use a plastic knife or Popsicle stick to cut the log into small pieces.

▶ Let him pour premeasured ingredients and stir whenever possible.

◀ Give him the lettuce to tear for a salad and the salad dressing to shake in a tightly closed plastic container.

The kitchen can be a great learning environment for your child, but the many irresistible things to see, touch, taste, and smell also make it a hazardous place for unsupervised children. Remember to always be safety-conscious. Make sure any dangerous objects are well out of reach, and be sure to closely supervise any use of sharp utensils, the oven, or the stove. Better yet, make a rule that only an adult can use those things.

The activities in this chapter suggest fun ways for toddlers to become involved in the preparation of food.

Letter Sandwiches

Alphabet cereal
Sliced wheat bread
Peanut butter, jam, or honey

Spread the slices of bread with peanut butter, jam, or honey. Help your older toddler spell his name or a simple sentence such as "I love you" by applying the appropriate alphabet letters to his slice of bread.

Younger toddlers will probably enjoy sticking the letters onto the bread, or they may not want to combine the two at all!

Picture Menus

If you like to give your child a choice at mealtime, but he tends to want the same meals day after day, picture menus may be the answer.

> Pictures of your child's favourite meals
> Heavy paper
> Glue
> Magnetic clip

Plan several different meals that you know your child likes, being sure to include fruit, vegetables, and a healthy snack in each one. Cut out pictures of each meal from grocery store flyers, coupons, product labels, or magazine pictures. Glue the pictures to index cards or pieces of heavy paper (one meal per page) and hang them on a magnetic clip on the refrigerator. After your child chooses a meal he'd like, move that card to a different location until all the cards have been used up, then start over. Your child still has a choice, but there will be less arguing, indecision, and monotony.

Pudding Paints

> Packaged pudding mix

Prepare packaged pudding mix ahead of time and, when cooled, allow your child to finger paint on a plastic or paper plate, tabletop, highchair tray, or other smooth surface. This may not be suitable before a meal, but there probably won't be much left to clean up!

Homemade Butter

> Heavy cream
> Baby food or other small jar with a tight-fitting lid
> Sieve or cheesecloth

Place the cream in the jar and cover it tightly with a lid. Your child can shake and shake and shake the jar until the cream forms soft lumps. Drain this through a sieve or cheesecloth and discard the liquid. Mash the remaining lumps in a bowl until they're smooth. Serve on muffins, bread, or crackers for a tasty snack.

Jell-O Paints

Two or three different colours of Jell-O

Prepare two or three different colours of Jell-O ahead of time. When set, place globs of each colour on a plastic or paper plate, tabletop, highchair tray, or other smooth surface. Your child will have fun mucking about with this tasty fingerpaint, and eating it will not harm him!

Butterfly Sandwiches

Bread
Cream cheese, peanut butter, or other bread spread
Bananas, raisins, pickles, vegetable slices

Create an open-faced butterfly sandwich by cutting a slice of bread diagonally then reversing the halves to form a butterfly. Spread with cream cheese, peanut butter, or other bread spread, then decorate with pickles, banana slices, raisins, or other pieces of soft fruit. Cut carrots or peppers in thin strips for antennae.

Fruit Dips

Long plastic straws
Fruit cut into chunks
Yogourt (optional)

Cut a variety of fruit into chunks. These could include orange cubes, pineapple pieces, apple squares, strawberry bites, peach parts, whole grapes (or halves for really young children), and banana chunks. Show your child how to slide the pieces onto a long plastic straw. Eat them as is or dip them into yogourt for a great tasting, fun-to-eat snack.

Dump Cake

This is the type of cake where even the youngest child can boast, "I made it all by myself."

> 540-ml (20-oz.) can crushed pineapple
> 450-ml (16-oz.) can cherry pie filling
> Yellow cake mix
> ¾ cup butter or margarine

Butter a 9-by-13-inch baking pan. Dump in the crushed pineapple, including the juice, and spread evenly. Spoon the cherry pie filling evenly over the pineapple. Sprinkle the yellow cake mix over the fruit. Slice the butter or margarine thinly and place the pieces on top of the cake mix. Bake at 350 degrees for 45 minutes.

Bananas, Honey, and Wheat Germ

This is a sticky activity, but a banana lover's delight!

> Banana
> Honey
> Milk
> Wheat germ
> Plastic knives or Popsicle sticks

Mix some honey with a little milk to thin it, then put it into a small bowl. Put some wheat germ into a second small bowl. Cut a banana in half and give your child a half to peel. Let him cut his banana half into smaller pieces with a plastic knife or Popsicle stick. Show him how to dip a banana chunk first into the honey bowl, then into the wheat germ. He may want to eat it right away, or you can place each dipped chunk on a small plate to save for later.

Apple Smiles

Apple
Peanut butter
Miniature marshmallows

Cut a crisp apple into slices, cutting vertically from the outside in towards the core. If the apple is red and unpeeled, each slice when turned horizontally should look like a lip. Spread one side of an apple slice with peanut butter. Add three or four miniature marshmallow "teeth" along the unpeeled edge. Spread another apple slice with peanut butter. Place it on top of the first apple slice for a big, toothy grin.

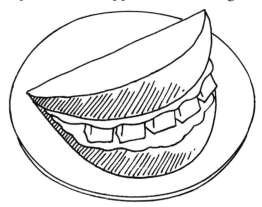

What Is It?

Scarf for blindfolding
Various objects to touch, smell, and taste

Challenge your child's senses by blindfolding him and giving him objects to identify using his sense of touch, smell, and taste. Very young children (or children who object to being blindfolded) can simply close their eyes. Start with something easy, such as a banana or cracker. Try nonfood items as well (a feather or a favourite toy), and be prepared to take a turn at the challenge yourself.

Vegetable Teethers

Frozen mixed vegetables

Serve your teething toddlers frozen mixed vegetables straight from the freezer. Most kids like them better uncooked, and they can be a quick fix for those fussy times.

No-Bake Banana Cookies

> Graham wafers
> Rolling pin
> Ziploc bag
> Bananas or other fruit

Place three graham wafers in a Ziploc bag and crush them with a rolling pin. Slice a banana or other fruit into small pieces. Shake a few pieces at a time in the bag to completely coat the fruit. Lay the pieces out on a plate and, if you like, add little forks for spearing.

Fruit Popsicles

> Baby food (puréed fruit)
> Unsweetened fruit juice

Empty a jar of baby food into a measuring cup. Add unsweetened fruit juice to make one cup. Stir well and pour into a four-section Popsicle mould. Insert handles and freeze until set. To double the recipe, add another cup of juice.

Mud Balls

> 1 cup peanut butter
> ¼ cup honey
> ½ cup dry, powdered milk
> ½ cup raisins
> Crushed graham wafers
> Chocolate milk powder

Mix all ingredients together in a medium-sized bowl. Show your toddler how to form the mixture into balls. Place a small amount of chocolate milk powder on a plate and roll the balls in the powder. Eat as a tasty snack or refrigerate and serve later.

Fruit Salad

Younger toddlers can help cut the bananas and perhaps the canned fruit with a plastic knife. They can also dump and mix the ingredients. Older toddlers can do most of the cutting with a dull knife. This recipe makes enough salad for a group of toddlers, so adjust the quantities as necessary.

    Canned peaches, pears, pineapple
    Bananas
    Apples
    Vanilla yogourt

Open some canned fruit (or use fresh if possible) and cut pieces small enough for toddlers to eat. Peel and slice bananas and apples. Mix it all in a large bowl with vanilla yogourt and serve to toddlers in small bowls.

Ants on A Log

This easy, no-bake treat is fun to make, and healthy, too!

    Celery sticks
    Small plastic knife or Popsicle stick
    Peanut butter
    Raisins

Wash and cut celery into 3- or 4-inch lengths. Give your child a small, plastic knife or a Popsicle stick and show him how to spread peanut butter onto the celery. Stick raisins in the peanut butter and eat. If your child has an allergy to peanut butter, use cheese spread, cream cheese, or even jam or honey.

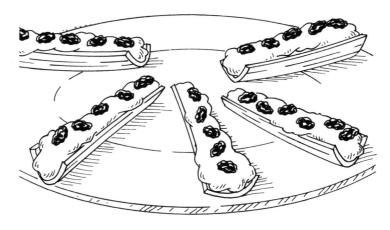

Peanut Butter Sculptures

I don't know which part of this activity children enjoy more: building the sculpture or eating it!

Peanut butter
Crackers
Small plastic knife or Popsicle stick

Put peanut butter onto a small plate or into a small plastic container (unless you don't mind your toddler sticking his fingers into the whole jar). If your child has an allergy to peanut butter, use cheese spread, cream cheese, jam, or honey. Show your child how to spread the peanut butter onto a cracker, then stick another cracker on top of it. Use a few different kinds of crackers if possible. Even animal crackers are fun.

Marshmallow Treats

These treats aren't very nutritional, but toddlers will love to help make their own, colourful snack.

Regular-sized marshmallows
Jell-O jelly powder
Ziploc bag

Pour some jelly powder inside a Ziploc bag. Insert a marshmallow or two, seal the bag, and shake. Remove the coated marshmallows from the bag and eat.

Washing Vegetables

Small basin of water
Vegetable brush or dish cloth
Vegetables or fruit to wash
Tea towel for drying

Fill a small basin with several inches of water. Give your child several pieces of fruit or vegetables to wash in the basin. He may enjoy using a vegetable brush or gently rubbing them with a dish cloth. When they are clean, show him how to dry the fruit or vegetables with a clean tea towel.

Pudding Cookies

These cookies require only a minimal amount of measuring, so they're easy to make when you have a toddler or two helping you. Let your child add the chocolate chips, raisins, or coconut by the spoonful or the handful.

> 1 cup Bisquick baking mix
> 1 small package instant pudding
> ¼ cup salad oil
> 1 egg
> ⅓ cup peanut butter (optional)
> Chocolate chips, raisins, coconut (optional)
> White sugar
> Cinnamon candies or chocolate chips for decorating (optional)

Combine baking mix, instant pudding, salad oil, and egg in a mixing bowl. If you like, add peanut butter, chocolate chips, raisins, and coconut. Roll the dough into balls and put them on an ungreased cookie sheet. Dip the bottom of a glass in sugar and press it on each ball until flattened. If making plain dough, cookies may be decorated with red cinnamon candies or chocolate chips before baking. Bake at 350 degrees for 8 minutes. Makes 2 to 3 dozen cookies.

Quickie Cookies

These cookies aren't very nutritious either, but older toddlers can practically make them on their own. There's no measuring if you use premeasured margarine squares, and cleanup will be a bowl, mixing spoon, and cookie sheets.

> 1 package cake mix
> ½ cup butter or margarine
> 1 egg

Mix all the ingredients in a medium-sized bowl. Mould into balls and place on greased cookie sheets. Bake at 350 degrees for about 10 minutes or until done. Cool for a few minutes on the cookie sheet, then remove to a cooling rack to cool completely.

Painted Toast

2 tablespoons milk
Food colouring
Clean paintbrush
White bread
Toaster

Mix the milk with a few drops of food colouring in a small container. Use a paintbrush to paint designs or faces on the bread. Toast the bread in a toaster. Butter and eat, or use to make a sandwich.

Apple Shake-Ups

Apple
Knife
Sugar
Cinnamon
Ziploc bag

Peel an apple and cut into toddler-sized pieces. Or cut it into larger slices and have your older toddler use a plastic knife to cut it into smaller pieces. Place a tablespoon or two of sugar and about a half-teaspoon of cinnamon into a Ziploc bag. Add a few apple pieces, seal the bag, and shake to coat the apples. Remove the coated apples from the bag and eat.

Zoo Sandwiches

Sliced bread
Cream cheese
Cream
Food colouring (optional)
Plastic knives
Animal cookie cutters

Combine cream cheese with cream in a mixing bowl, using about one tablespoon of cream per three ounces of cream cheese. Mix with a spoon until the cream cheese is soft. Add a few drops of food colouring, if desired, and stir well. Cut animal-shaped pieces of bread with the animal cookie cutters. Use a small plastic knife or Popsicle stick to spread the cream cheese mixture on the bread.

If your child is not fond of cream cheese, use peanut butter, honey, or jam instead.

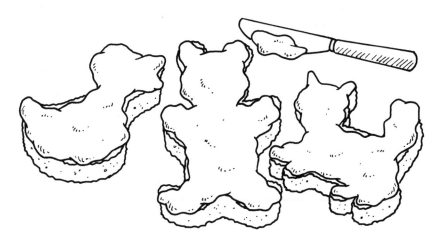

CHAPTER FOUR

Water Play

A lot of people assume that because I am the mother of ten children I must be an expert on motherhood, but such is not the case. It is true that I have learned a great deal over the years, but fortunately I have managed to forget most of what I have learned. (That is how I stayed sane.)

TERESA BLOOMINGDALE

FOR YOUNG CHILDREN, WATER ISN'T JUST FOR GETTING CLEAN. IN FACT, water play for toddlers is rarely about getting clean. Dumping, pouring, filling, mixing … playing with sponges, corks, cups, bowls, soap, ice cubes, and so on, is a lot of fun for toddlers and preschoolers. It also encourages discovery and stimulates interest in the physical world.

Water play can also help parents and other caregivers maintain their sanity. During the early months of my third pregnancy, my two-year-old and one-year-old happily played in the bath on many rainy mornings. It was a great way for them to have fun while I did as little as possible!

Most toddlers probably have at least one water play session each day—bath time. Here are a few suggestions to help your child get the maximum amount of fun out of every bath.

- ▲ Put a few inches of water in the tub, place your child in the water, then leave the tap run slowly so your child can fill up cups, play in the stream of water, and so on.
- ◄ Add as many plastic kitchen utensils as you can spare to your collection of bath toys.
- ▶ Sponges (plain or cut into shapes) are fun for the bath.
- ◄ A Ping-Pong ball is lots of fun in the tub. Try to keep it under the water—it will always pop up!

- ▼ Toddlers will love filling up small containers with water.
- ▶ Add inflated balloons, corks, or ice cubes to the bath (supervise carefully to prevent choking on small items or bits of broken balloon).
- ◀ Poke a few holes in the bottom of a plastic container such as a margarine tub. Children will enjoy filling it with water and watching the water drip and dribble out the bottom.
- ▼ Make up a batch of Bubble Solution (see Chapter 5) and blow bubbles as your child has her bath.

If your toddler is like mine, she loves to line up her little cups and other containers along the edge of the bathtub and then repeatedly fill them up, dump them out, and fill them up again. While great fun for children, this activity usually results in a lot of water on the bathroom floor (and, in some cases, a lot of water leaking through to the ceiling of the room below). A small, Rubbermaid-type step stool placed in the bathtub gives your child a great platform for her containers and helps keep most of the water in the tub.

Water play is also a great kitchen activity. Most toddlers will enjoy standing on a chair at the kitchen sink and playing in a sinkful of water with bowls, cups, and other containers. If you have a dishwasher in your kitchen, the open door of a clean, empty dishwasher makes a great water play table for your toddler. Simply add a bucket of water and some small cups and containers to fill and dump. A thick towel in front of the sink or under the open dishwasher door will help to soak up spills.

The following ideas for water play cover a variety of situations—both indoors and out. You may find some of these ideas better suited to older toddlers and preschoolers. Remember, drowning in a water-filled bucket or a few inches of water in the bathtub is a very real possibility for toddlers, so please supervise any water play carefully.

Wash the Floor

Sponge

Give your child a wet sponge and let her help you when you're washing the floor. Once you know she will not automatically dump it, give her an inch or two of water in a small bucket or bowl. She will have fun being your helper, and cleanup is easy!

Fun with Water

If you don't mind water all over the floor, you can use this idea inside. Otherwise, you may want to save it for a warm day outdoors. Young toddlers tend to have more fun dumping the bucket rather than playing with the dishes and utensils, so try using a bucket that, when filled, is too heavy for them to lift (a large, clean, empty laundry- or dishwasher-detergent container works well).

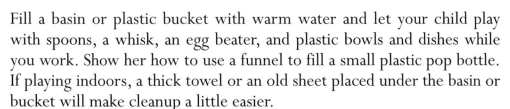

Large plastic basin or bucket
Various kitchen utensils: spoons, egg beater, whisk, and so on
Plastic bowls and dishes
Small plastic bottles
Funnel

Fill a basin or plastic bucket with warm water and let your child play with spoons, a whisk, an egg beater, and plastic bowls and dishes while you work. Show her how to use a funnel to fill a small plastic pop bottle. If playing indoors, a thick towel or an old sheet placed under the basin or bucket will make cleanup a little easier.

Cork Race

You will need one of each of the following items for each player. Many toddlers haven't yet mastered the skill of blowing through a straw—you may want to save this idea for when they're a little older.

Cork
9-by-13-inch baking pan
Straw

Fill each baking pan with water and place them on a table or on the floor. Give each player a cork and a straw. The winner is the first one to blow her cork from one side of the pan to the other.

Waterfall Game

Pennies
Bowl, cup, or other container
Water

Fill a container almost to the top with water. Give each player a supply of pennies. Take turns dropping a penny into the container. The game ends when one player drops in the penny that makes the water overflow.

Soap Crayons

These are fun to write with in the tub or to use when washing little hands.

1½ cups pure soap powder (Ivory Snow)
Food colouring
½ cup water
Small containers or ice cube tray

Mix water and soap powder together. Add enough food colouring to get the colour you want. If you'd like more than one colour, divide the mixture into two or three small containers before adding food colouring. Pour the coloured soap into a small container (empty plastic film canisters work well) or an ice cube tray, or mould it into crayon shapes and let harden before using.

Michelangelo's Bathroom

Try this idea if your child hates getting water on her face when you wash her hair.

Colourful pictures
Tape

Tape some colourful pictures to the ceiling over your bathtub (old calendars are a great source for these). Your child can look at the pictures and talk with you about them as you wash her hair. Unless she has a favourite, change the pictures often to maintain interest.

Bathtime Bubbles

Bubble solution
Bubble blower

Blow bubbles for your child while she sits in the bath. Have her try to catch them in her open hands or clap her hands together to pop them.

Drown the Penny

Paper towel
Glass filled with water
Pencil
Elastic
Penny

Place the paper towel over the water-filled glass. Wrap an elastic band around the top of the glass to hold the paper towel in place. Place the penny on the paper towel in the centre of the glass. Take turns poking holes in the paper towel with the pencil. The game ends when someone "drowns the penny" by poking the hole that finally makes the penny sink to the bottom of the glass.

Bathtub Soap Paint

You may not want to use this idea if your child has sensitive skin.

> ½ cup pure soap flakes (Ivory Snow)
> ¾ cup water
> Food colouring
> Electric mixer or wire whisk
> Paintbrush
> Spray bottle

Use an electric mixer or wire whisk to whip the soap flakes and water together until you get the texture of shaving cream. Add food colouring (be careful—it can stain the grout around ceramic tiles and should be omitted if this worries you). Use a brush to paint the wall around the bathtub. Give your child a spray bottle filled with water and let her spray the paint off.

Water Play

This bathtime variation is great for long, rainy days.

> Plastic baby bath
> Bath toys

Sit your diapered child in an empty bathtub. Fill a plastic baby bath or other large container with water and set it beside your child. Provide an assortment of bath toys that she can play with (cups, spoons, bowls, funnels, empty squeeze bottles, a plastic teapot, and sponges all make excellent water play toys).

Sponge Play

> Sponges
> Water
> Two bowls or other containers

Fill one bowl with water and add a few drops of food colouring if you like. Show your toddler how to place the sponge in the bowl full of water, then transfer the water to the empty bowl by squeezing the sponge.

Coloured Ice Cubes

While ice cubes will melt fairly quickly in a warm bath, they can still be a choking hazard for little ones. Please supervise carefully.

> Ice cube tray
> Water
> Food colouring

Make coloured ice cubes by adding a drop of food colouring to the water in each section of an ice cube tray. Freeze. Add a bowl of different coloured ice cubes to the bath for some bathtime fun.

Rock Drop

> Wading pool, large bucket, or dishpan
> Water
> Rocks large enough to pass the choke test

Put a few inches of water in a wading pool, large bucket, or dishpan, and let your toddler drop the rocks into the water.

Ice Blocks

If small ice cubes melt too quickly, make a larger block of ice to play with in the bath or outside on a warm summer day.

> Clean cardboard milk carton
> Water
> Food colouring (optional)
> Small plastic toys (optional)

Make an ice block by freezing water in a clean cardboard milk carton. If you like, add a few drops of food colouring to the water before freezing, or drop in a few small plastic toys. Place in the freezer until frozen. Your child will enjoy playing with the block in the bath or outside in the pool. If you've frozen small plastic toys inside the block, watch your child's surprise as the ice melts and the toys appear.

As a variation, fill balloons with water, tie tightly, and freeze to make ice balls.

Toddler Sprinkler

This idea may become a real hit around your house (outside, of course!).

> Large plastic bottle (4-litre milk jugs work great)
> Hammer and nail

Use a hammer and nail to poke holes in the bottom of a large plastic bottle. When you're outside, fill the bottle with water and let your child sprinkle the grass, flowers, sidewalk, driveway, and so on.

Water Rhythms

A toddler with a hose will have a good time, no doubt about it. Upside-down pots add a dimension of sound for some extra fun.

> Metal pots and lids
> Garden hose with spray attachment

Turn the pots upside down on the grass or driveway. Prop up some of the pot lids against a wall or fence. Turn on the water and let your toddler spray the pots and lids to hear the drumming noises.

Baster Play

In *Surviving Your Preschooler*, I suggest this activity using an eye dropper. Toddlers will enjoy doing the same with a large baster.

Kitchen baster
Plastic bowls or other containers
Water

Fill one bowl with water; add a few drops of food colouring if you like. Show your toddler how to place the baster in the bowl full of water and squeeze the bulb. She will enjoy watching the tube fill up with water. Show her how to hold the baster over an empty container and let go of the bulb to release the water.

Ice Play

This is a great outdoor idea for a hot day. If you'd rather do this inside, sit your toddler in an empty bathtub with the pan of ice beside her.

Crushed ice
Plastic dishpan or large bowl
Bath toys

Put some crushed ice into a plastic dishpan or large plastic bowl. Your child will have fun using her bath toys (cups, spoons, bowls, and so on) to play with the ice. If you're making the ice beforehand, add a few drops of food colouring to the water before freezing it.

Car Wash

Bucket of warm, soapy water
Cloth or sponge
Hose
Riding toys

Help your child set up a toddler car wash. Give her a bucket of warm, soapy water, and a cloth or sponge, and let her wash her riding toys. She may need help using the hose to rinse them when she's finished.

Gone Fishing

Large bucket or dishpan
Water
Plastic fish-bait worms
Scoop or small strainer (optional)
Corks, Ping-Pong balls, small sponge scraps (optional)

Fill a large bucket or dishpan with water. Add a few plastic fish-bait worms and let your toddler have fun trying to catch them in her hands or in a scoop or small strainer. For variety, float corks, Ping-Pong balls, or small sponge scraps in the water. Encourage your toddler to scoop them out one by one.

Target Practice

This is a great game for a summer get-together or birthday party. If your child isn't old enough to shoot a watergun, use the garden hose instead.

1-litre (32 oz.) plastic pop bottles (three or four)
Ping-Pong balls
Water gun or garden hose

Fill three or four plastic pop bottles with water. Set the bottles on a level surface (a child's picnic table works well). Place a Ping-Pong ball on top of each bottle. Use the watergun or garden hose to try to shoot the balls off the bottles.

Coloured Sand

> Spray bottle
> Water
> Food colouring or liquid paint

Fill a spray bottle with water and add a few drops of food colouring or a few spoonfuls of liquid paint. Let your child spray the sand in the sand-box to make a colourful desert. Turn the sand over with a shovel and watch the colour disappear. Now your child can start all over again.

Ball Splash

> Wading pool
> Water
> Large beach ball

Fill a wading pool with a few inches of water. Face your toddler across the pool and take turns throwing a beach ball hard at the water, trying to splash each other and yourself.

Wet the Chalkboard

> Chalkboard
> Sponge or large paintbrush
> Water

Encourage your child to paint or wipe the chalkboard with a wet sponge or large paintbrush dipped in water. She will enjoy seeing it darken as it gets wet.

Sponge Tag

> Sponges
> Bucket of water

Soak sponges in water, then have fun throwing them at each other. If your child doesn't like the idea of being the target, try throwing sponges at a tree or garage door, or use sidewalk chalk to draw a big circle or other shape and aim for that instead.

Water Balloon Catch

Balloons
Water

Fill several balloons with water and play catch with them, or use side-walk chalk to draw a target on the sidewalk and aim for that instead. Be sure to pick up any broken balloon pieces promptly, as they pose a serious choking hazard for young children.

Funnels and Tubes

12- to 18-inch length of ½-inch flexible plastic tubing
Funnel
Plastic measuring cup or small container
Dishpan or large bucket
Food colouring

Fill the dishpan or large bucket with water. Add a few drops of food colouring to make coloured water. Attach a funnel to one end of the flexible plastic tubing (if it doesn't stay securely, you may want to use a glue gun to permanently attach the two together). Place the other end of the tubing in the dishpan or bucket. Show your toddler how to scoop up some water from the bucket and pour it into the funnel. She will enjoy watching the coloured water flow through the tubing and back into the bucket. If you like, use two buckets and have her transfer water from one bucket to another with her cup, funnel, and tubing.

CHAPTER FIVE

Outdoor Adventures

As soon as I stepped out of my mother's womb on to dry land, I realized that I had made a mistake—that I shouldn't have come, but the trouble with children is that they are not returnable.

QUENTIN CRISP

OUTDOOR PLAY EVERY DAY, IN ALMOST ANY WEATHER, IS ESSENTIAL FOR children of all ages. Whether playing in the snow, picking spring flowers, crunching fall leaves, or stomping in puddles after a rain, toddlers need to be outdoors to master their newfound skills of walking, running, climbing, and jumping.

Whatever the weather, toddlers will almost certainly find something to amuse themselves with. Most never tire of sand and water play, and swings and slides are a great deal of fun as well as a great way to work off some of their seemingly endless energy. Whether you push a stroller, pull a wagon, or walk with your child at a toddler's pace, both parent and child will benefit from short walks outdoors almost every day.

The ideas in this chapter will provide some fun and interesting things to do with your toddler outdoors. Most require a minimum of materials, and you will find that, with minor changes, most are suitable for any season and any weather. Many indoor-play ideas in Chapter 2 or water-play ideas in Chapter 4 are also easily adaptable to outdoor play.

Leaf Scrunch

Dry leaves
Small box
Clear contact paper (optional)

Collect dry leaves in a bag on an autumn walk with your child. At home, dump the leaves into a box and let your child scrunch the leaves with his hands. If you like, use some of the colourful pieces to make a fall collage on a piece of clear contact paper.

Measuring Magic

Measuring cups and spoons
Bowls or small containers
Water, sand, or mud

Give your child an assortment of cups, spoons, bowls, and other containers and let him play outdoors with water, sand, or mud.

Mud Handprints

Mud
Sturdy paper or plastic plate
Spatula or knife for smoothing

Fill the plate with thick mud and smooth into a flat, even surface. Have your child press his open hand into the mud and remove. Place the mud in the sun to dry. This won't last, but it's fun to look at for awhile. For lasting prints, use plaster of Paris.

Jell-O Jumping

4 large packages of Jell-O
Baby bathtub

Prepare Jell-O according to package directions. Place it in a baby's bathtub or small basin and let your child stand in it, sit in it, run his fingers through it, or paint with it.

Red, Red, Red

You can play this game with a group of children, or when it's just you and your child.

Have the players stand next to each other behind a starting line. The leader calls out three colours (for example, "Red, red, red!"). If the colours don't match ("Red, red, yellow!"), no one moves. If the colours do match, then children run, skip, or hop to a distant point and back. Feel free to substitute animals ("Cat, cat, dog!"), body parts ("Hand, hand, foot!"), or whatever you like.

Frog in the Grass

Four green rubber frogs (or rubber snakes, beanbags, or small plastic toys)

Have your child stand on the far side of the yard and close his eyes. Hide the frogs in the grass in different spots around the yard. When you yell, "Frog in the grass!" your child must run and find the frogs. Make sure he grabs them before they hop away!

Nature Bracelet

Masking tape
Scissors

Before going outdoors with your child, wrap a piece of masking tape to his wrist, sticky side up. As you explore, help him attach colourful leaves, flowers, and other interesting discoveries to his bracelet. When done, use scissors to snip off the nature bracelet. Display on a bulletin board, shelf, or wall.

BUBBLE SOLUTION

The following three bubble-solution recipes come from Science World in Vancouver, British Columbia. They say the following about glycerine: "Not all detergents require the addition of glycerine in order to make good soap solutions. Glycerine helps soap bubbles hold water and this helps to keep the bubbles from popping. Try a tablespoon or two for a small batch (we're not exact about it). Glycerine can be purchased at most pharmacies. You won't need much, so don't go buying caseloads."

All-purpose Bubble Solution

Here's a good all-purpose solution for most bubble tricks, experiments, and activities.

> 7 to 10 parts water
> 1 part dish detergent
> Glycerine

Combine water, detergent, and a tablespoon or two of glycerine (see note above) in a bowl or plastic container.

Bouncy Bubble Solution

This is a fun solution that you can bounce off your clothes.

> 2 packages unflavored gelatine
> 4 cups hot water (just boiled)
> 3 to 5 tablespoons glycerine
> 3 tablespoons dish detergent

Dissolve the gelatine in hot water. Add glycerine and dish detergent. This mixture will gel, so you'll need to reheat it whenever you use it.

Thick Bubble Solution

This is a very thick, goopy solution that forms bubbles strong enough to withstand a small puff of air. You can blow bubbles inside of bubbles with this mixture and you don't need a straw. Just make a bubble and blow!

2½ to 3 parts water
1 part dish detergent
Glycerine

Combine water, detergent, and a tablespoon or two of glycerine (see note above) in a bowl or plastic container.

Bubble Fun

Plastic drinking straws
Store-bought or home-made bubble solution (see Bubble Solution, this chapter)
Scissors
Tape

Make a bubble wand by cutting two plastic drinking straws in half, then taping the four pieces together. Blowing through the straws will send lots of tiny bubbles in many directions.

Dodge Ball

This is a fun game for four or more children.

Large, soft ball (try crumpled up newspaper and tape, or onion-bag netting stuffed with cotton balls or batting)

Have children form a circle with one child in the middle. Each player in the outer circle takes a turn throwing the ball at the child in the middle, who tries to dodge out of the way. When the child in the middle gets hit, he changes places with the child who hit him.

Toddler Ball

Plastic ball
Plastic bat and tee (optional)

Show your child how to throw or kick a plastic ball, or have him try hitting it with a plastic bat off a tee. Pick up the ball and chase your child to a "base" (a tree or other designated point) and then back to "home." You may want to tag your child occasionally, but let him try being "safe" sometimes, too.

Balloon Kites

Flying a kite is difficult and frustrating for toddlers and preschoolers. These "kites" are guaranteed to fly, even on days with light wind.

Large, round helium balloons
Kite string
Paper streamers (optional)

Tie one end of a long length of kite string to a round helium balloon and the other to your child's wrist. He will find it fun and easy to fly his balloon, and you won't worry about crashes and tangles. Attach lengths of paper streamers to the balloon to give it a more authentic kite look.

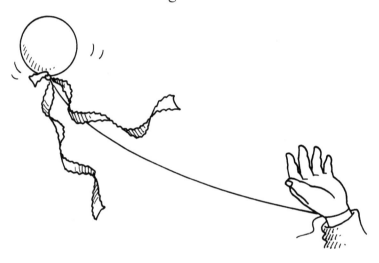

Spaghetti Splash

We tried this in our backyard one warm summer day as part of our playgroup wind-up. Although many years have passed, my children and the parents who attended still talk about it! Watch out, though, it can kill the grass!

2-3 packages cooked spaghetti
⅓ cup vegetable oil
Food colouring
Child's wading pool

Mix all ingredients in a child's wading pool. Children may want to play with the spaghetti with their hands, sit in it, or (as we tried) use a small slide to get right into the middle of it.

Shadow Tracing

Chalk

Go outside with your child on a sunny day. If your child will stand still long enough, trace his shadow on the sidewalk or driveway. Have him change positions, then trace his shadow again. Make several shadow tracings, then see if he can fit himself back inside his shadow.

For a fun alternative, trace his shadow on a big sheet of newsprint or other paper. Let him fingerpaint his shadow or colour it with crayons or markers.

Teddy Swing

Rope, heavy string, or ribbon
Teddy bear or favourite stuffed animal

Tie one end of a length of rope, heavy string, or ribbon around the middle of your child's favourite teddy bear or other stuffed animal. Tie the other end of the rope to a tree branch so that teddy is about two feet off the ground. Your child will have fun pushing his teddy to make him swing.

Rope Games

This activity is good for either indoor or outdoor play.

Long rope

Lay a long rope in a zigzag pattern in the grass or on your deck. See if your child can walk on the rope. Lay the rope in a straight line like a tightrope and have your child hold out his arms to balance himself as he walks. With the rope still lying straight, ask your child to think of how many ways he can go over it: walk across it, hop over it (on one or two feet), jump across it, crawl across it, or any other way he can think of.

Digging for Treasure

Small objects to hide
Shovels
Colander
Sandbox

Hide small objects in the sandbox for your toddler to find as he digs about. Use an old kitchen colander to sift through the sand. If you like, spray paint rocks in shiny silver and gold, and show your toddler how to search for hidden treasure.

Changing Colours

This is a good activity for outdoors or in, and will also entertain children on a long car ride.

Coloured cellophane in various colours

Give your child a piece of coloured cellophane. Go for a walk outside and encourage your child to look at familiar objects through the cellophane. Your child will enjoy seeing how the colour of everyday objects changes when seen through the cellophane. If you like, change the colour of cellophane your child is using, or look through two pieces of cellophane at the same time to see how the colours change yet again.

Snow Painting

You'll have the prettiest yard in the neighbourhood after this activity!

Spray bottle
Water
Food colouring or liquid tempera paint

Fill a spray bottle with water and add a few drops of food colouring, or a spoon or two of liquid tempera paint. Dress your child warmly and take him ouside to "paint" the snow with his spray bottle. Children will also enjoy using brushes and liquid tempera paint to paint the snow.

Window Painting

Adding a little dish detergent to the fingerpaint makes cleanup easier!

Fingerpaint
Dish detergent (optional)
Wet paintbrush or cotton swab (optional)

On a warm day outdoors, let your child fingerpaint on the outside of a glass patio door or low window. When the paint dries, use a wet paintbrush or cotton swab dipped in water to make a design on the paint. Cleaning up with a sponge and bucket of water or garden hose can be part of the fun.

Crayon Slide

If you have a slide in your backyard (or a small one indoors), this activity will add a new dimension to sliding fun.

Slide
Newspaper or long length of paper
Tape
Crayons

Tape a length of newspaper to your child's slide. Give him one or two crayons (perhaps one for each hand) and have him slide down the slide, holding the crayons to the paper as he goes. He will enjoy seeing the squiggly lines and designs he's made. Change colours and keep sliding until your child tires of this activity.

If you like, bundle up three or four (or more) crayons with an elastic band for a different effect.

CHAPTER SIX

Out and About

Children are a great comfort in your old age—and they help you reach it faster, too.
                                                         LIONEL M. KAUFFMAN

MOST CHILDREN, NO MATTER THEIR AGE, WOULD RATHER BE PLAYING and moving about than sitting still for an extended period of time. Also, toddlers are fairly limited in their language skills and ability to play games and carry out independent activities. For these reasons, long car rides and waits in the doctor's office can be especially frustrating for those running errands with a toddler in tow.

There are, however, simple things you can do to help your child through these challenging situations. Provide her with her very own Busy Bag (see Chapter 1) and fill it with toddler-appropriate items. Bring along her favourite book, toy, or snack to help her through times when you're forced to sit and wait. Sing songs, recite nursery rhymes, and learn some simple finger plays to keep her attention (see Chapter 7).

The ideas in this chapter are great for those times when your toddler just has to sit. The simple games and activities will help keep her entertained and happy, and many may become favourites for other times as well.

What Would Happen If ...?

This is a great activity to promote creative thinking in young children. Ask your child some "What would happen if ..." questions. For example, "What would happen if the dinosaurs came back?" or "What would happen if cars could fly?" or "What would happen if broccoli tasted like chocolate?" or "What would happen if all the trees were red?" and so on.

What Would You Be?

You can encourage your older two- or three-year-old to use her imagination by playing games such as this. Ask your child, "If you could spend one day as an animal, which one would you be?" and "What do you think your day might be like?" You may want to give your child some examples, or start the game off yourself, pretending to be a dog digging for a bone, or a baby bird in the nest waiting for Mommy to return.

Where Is It?

As you're driving in the car, name things that you see and ask your toddler to point to them (for example, "Where is the tree?"). If you're waiting in a place where your child can move around, ask her to walk over to the object you name.

Colour of the Day

Before you set out on a car trip, choose a "Colour of the Day." As you're driving in the car, shopping at the grocery store, or waiting at the doctor's office, help your toddler point to and identify all the things she sees that match the colour you've chosen.

Ask a Question

While riding in the car or waiting for your meal at a restaurant, take a few minutes to ask your child some questions. Try to avoid yes/no questions and encourage your child to give reasons for her answers. Some of her responses may be hilarious, but you'll be surprised at what you can learn about your child if you take the time to really listen to the answers she gives. Here are a few questions to start you off.

- ▲ Who is your best friend?
- ◄ Where does money come from?
- ▶ What is the best thing about Daddy (or Mommy)?
- ◄ What is the nicest thing that has ever happened to you?
- ▼ What is your favourite thing to do?
- ▶ When does God sleep?

Car Book

Old magazines
Scissors
Construction paper
Glue
Clear contact paper
Hole punch
Ribbon

Look through old magazines for pictures of cars or other vehicles. Cut out the pictures and glue them to pieces of construction paper. Protect the pages by covering them with clear contact paper. Punch two or three holes in the left margin of each page, then thread ribbon through the holes to make a book. (If you like, use a ring binder or staple the pages together.)

Give your child her car book to look through as you drive along. Ask her questions as she looks at the pages. For example, "Can you find a blue car?" or "Can you find a truck?" and so on.

Nursery Rhyme Fun

As you drive along, recite a familiar nursery rhyme or sing a familiar song to your child. When you get to a rhyming word, stop and see if your toddler can say or sing the correct word. For example, say, "Hickory, dickory, dock, the mouse ran up the _____" or "Little Jack Horner sat in a _____" or "Jack, be nimble, Jack be quick, Jack jump over the _____."

Shopping List

This word game may be beyond most one- and two-year-olds, but older two- and three-year-olds will love it.

As you drive along, say to your child, "I went to the store and I bought carrots, cabbage, and cream. What else did I buy?" Your child must add items to your shopping list that begin with the same sound as the items you have named. You can tell your child the rule for adding items (that they must begin with the same sound), or let older children figure it out for themselves. If they try to add something that doesn't begin with the same sound, tell them, "No, that wasn't on my list." They'll probably guess the rule after a few tries, but if they have trouble, keep adding items to your list until they understand.

Sandpaper Play

This is a clean, quiet activity that travels well. Store sandpaper and yarn in a Ziploc bag and have it handy for a long car ride or whenever you need something quick for your child to do.

> Coarse sandpaper
> Yarn in various colours
> Scissors

Cut various colours of yarn into different lengths. Show your toddler how the yarn sticks to the sandpaper. She will enjoy creating a design, pulling it off, and starting over again.

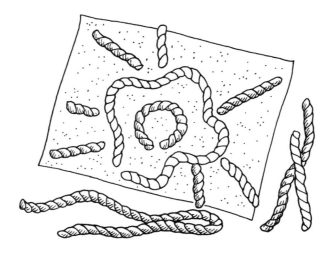

Stop and Go

Red and green construction paper
Scissors
Tape
Straw

Cut two circles from the red and green construction paper. Tape a straw to the back of each circle, leaving enough straw extending below the circle for your child to hold on to. Give your child the circles to hold in the car.

As you drive up to a red light, say to your child, "I'm stopping now because the light is red. Can you hold up your red light?" When the light turns green, say, "I'm starting to drive now because the light is green. Can you hold up your green light?" If you like, refer to your child's red and green lights as red and green circles to reinforce the concept of shape.

You can also play this game by cutting a stop sign from red construction paper. Tape a straw to the back, give it to your child, and ask her to hold her sign up every time you stop.

Felt Faces

Cardboard
Scissors
Felt
Glue
Pen or marker
Ziploc bag, diaper-wipe container, or small shoebox for storage

Cut several oval shapes out of cardboard. Trace around these shapes on pieces of felt (since these will be faces, felt in a variety of skin colours is desirable, but brightly coloured felt will work, too). Cut out the felt shapes you have traced and glue them to the cardboard ovals. Cut additional facial features from the felt in a variety of colours. These features should include eyes, nose, mouth (smiling and frowning), ears (with and without earrings, if you like), and hair. Older children may enjoy using additional features such as eyebrows, eyeglasses, moustaches, and so on.

Place the felt pieces (oval face shapes and facial features) in a Ziploc bag, empty diaper-wipe container, or small shoebox. This makes a clean and quiet take along game to play in the car or while you're waiting.

Take-Along Tape

Tape recorder with microphone
Cassette tape

Spend some time on your own making a tape for your toddler. Include familiar household sounds, sounds of animals, outdoor sounds, voices that the child will recognize, and so on. As you drive along, play the tape for your toddler and ask her to guess the sounds she hears.

As a variation, choose a story that your child is familiar with and read it on tape. As you read, make some mistakes, changing words in obvious places throughout the story. Have your child listen to the tape and pick out the errors.

Toddler Brag Book

This little homemade photo album slips easily into the diaper bag and comes in handy during long car rides or waiting times such as in a restaurant or doctor's office.

Photos of friends, family, pets, and your toddler
Construction paper
Glue
Clear contact paper
Scissors
Hole punch
Ribbon

Glue photos of your child and her friends, family, and pets to pieces of construction paper. Cover them with clear contact paper and cut to size, leaving a border of at least one-half inch around the photo. Punch two holes in the left margin of each page. Thread ribbon through the holes to make a "brag book." Your child will enjoy looking at this over and over.

If you like, use a small store-bought photo album (one photo per page) instead of making one with construction and contact paper.

CHAPTER SEVEN

Nursery Rhymes and Finger Plays

There never was a child so lovely but his mother was glad to get him asleep.

RALPH WALDO EMERSON

NURSERY RHYMES AND FINGER PLAYS CAN BE USED IN MANY DIFFERENT circumstances. You can use them on walks with your toddler or driving in the car. They will amuse your child at changing time or while he waits for his meal in his highchair. Sing or say the rhymes and finger plays as you rock in the rocking chair or as your child plays in his bath. Nursery rhymes and finger plays are appropriate just about anytime and anywhere.

In her book *Baby Games* (Stoddart Publishing Company, Toronto, ON, 1988), Elaine Martin says, "A common criticism of traditional nursery fare is that it is violent. Much of it is violent, aggressive, and full of surprises. While recognizing human gentleness, there is also an acknowledgement of the all-too-real capacity for human evil." While Martin goes on to explain that the nature of such rhymes allows us to resolve underlying conflicts in our lives in an appropriate way, many parents will not be comfortable reciting these nursery rhymes to their children. A book such as *The New Adventures of Mother Goose* by Bruce Lansky (Meadowbrook Press, Minnetonka, MN, 1993), and the rhymes and finger plays that follow provide a gentle alternative to frightening nursery rhymes.

To help you learn the words of any song or rhyme you're not familiar with, begin by reciting two lines at a time, repeating those lines throughout the day until you know them by heart. Add another two lines and continue in this way until the whole rhyme is memorized. Posting one or two unfamiliar rhymes around your baby's change table, on the wall next to the rocking chair, or on the kitchen wall close to his highchair will also help you learn them. You'll know them well after reading and saying them to your toddler several times.

Slowly, Slowly

Use your hands to mime the actions suggested by the words, or just use the rhyme as a tickling game with baby.

> Slowly, slowly, very slowly
> Creeps the garden snail.
> Slowly, slowly, very slowly
> Up the wooden rail.
>
> Quickly, quickly, very quickly
> Runs the little mouse.
> Quickly, quickly, very quickly
> Round about the house.

Two Little Eyes

Point to each feature as it is mentioned.

> Two little eyes to look around;
> Two little ears to hear each sound;
> One little nose to smell what's sweet;
> One little mouth that likes to eat.

Ten Little Gentlemen

Use your fingers to represent the gentlemen in this rhyme. When the door closes at the end, be sure to give a big clap.

> Ten little gentlemen, standing in a row.
> Bow, little gentlemen, bow down low;
> Walk, little gentlemen, right across the floor,
> And don't forget, gentlemen, to please close the door.

Round and Round the Garden

For the second verse, repeat the actions given for the first.

> Round and round the garden *(Run your index finger around baby's palm.)*
> Went the Teddy Bear,
> One step, two steps, *(Jump your finger up his arm.)*
> Tickle under there. *(Tickle him under his arm.)*
>
> Round and round the haystack,
> Went the little mouse,
> One step, two steps,
> In his little house.

Happy Days

Point to each feature as it is mentioned.

> Two eyes to see nice things to do;
> Two lips to smile the whole day through;
> Two ears to hear what others say;
> Two hands to put the toys away;
> A tongue to speak sweet words each day;
> A loving heart for work and play;
> Two feet that errands gladly run,
> Make happy days for everyone.

I Touch My Head

Follow the directions in the verse.

> I touch my head,
> I touch my toes.
> I shake my hands,
> Just see them go!
> I fold my arms,
> I cross my feet.
> I nod three times,
> I take a seat.

Mix a Pancake

Mime each action as you say it.

> Mix a pancake,
> Stir a pancake,
> Pop it in the pan.
>
> Fry the pancake,
> Toss the pancake,
> Catch it if you can!

Grandmother's Glasses

Make appropriate actions to fit the words as you say them. For glasses, join the thumb and forefinger on each hand. Use a higher voice for Grandmother, a deeper voice for Grandfather.

> These are Grandmother's glasses,
> This is Grandmother's hat;
> Grandmother claps her hands like this,
> And folds them in her lap.
>
> These are Grandfather's glasses,
> This is Grandfather's hat;
> This is the way he folds his arms,
> And has a little nap.

Here's a Ball for Baby

Here's a ball for baby, *(Make a ball with cupped hands.)*
Big and soft and round.
Here is baby's hammer, *(Hammer with one fist.)*
See how he can pound.

Here is baby's music, *(Clap hands.)*
Clapping, clapping, so.
Here are baby's soldiers, *(Hold fingers up straight.)*
Standing in a row.

Here is his umbrella, *(Hold hands above head.)*
To keep our baby dry.
Here is baby's cradle, *(Fold arms together and rock them.)*
To rock-a-baby-bye.

I Hear Thunder

This is sung to the tune of "Frère Jacques," or "Are You Sleeping?".

I hear thunder, I hear thunder; *(Drum feet on the floor.)*
Hark, don't you? Hark, don't you? *(Pretend to listen.)*
Pitter-patter raindrops, *(Flutter your fingers for raindrops.)*
Pitter-patter raindrops,
I'm wet through, *(Shake your body vigorously.)*
So are you! *(Point to your child.)*

Little Pussy Cats

One, two, three, four, *(Hold up four fingers from the right hand and count them.)*
These little pussy cats came to my door.
They just stood there and said "Good day," *(Make the fingers bow on "Good day.")*
And then they tiptoed right away. *(Walk the fingers away over the front of the body and behind the left shoulder.)*

Walking Through the Jungle

Pretend to walk very carefully through the jungle and mime the actions to suggest each animal. It's easy to make up more verses for this rhyme.

Walking through the jungle,
What did I see?
A big lion roaring
At me, me, me!

Walking through the jungle,
What did I see?
A baby monkey laughing
At me, me, me!

Walking through the jungle,
What did I see?
A slippery snake hissing
At me, me, me!

Snowflakes

Mime the actions suggested by the words.

> Softly, softly falling so,
> This is how the snowflakes go.
> Pitter-patter, pitter-patter,
> Pit pit pat,
> Down go the raindrops
> On my hat.

Five Little Mice

Use the fingers of one hand for the mice and the other hand for the cat. Continue each verse with one less mouse until there are no little mice scampering back.

> Five little mice came out to play,
> Gathering crumbs up on their way;
> Out came a pussy-cat, sleek and black—
> Four little mice went scampering back.
>
> Four little mice came out to play
> Gathering crumbs up on their way;
> Out came a pussy-cat, sleek and black—
> Three little mice went scampering back.
>
> Three little mice came out to play …

Marching Song

This song is sung to the tune of "Twinkle, Twinkle, Little Star." March around the room, either in separate directions or following the leader, as you sing it.

> See the soldiers in the street,
> Hear the marching of their feet;
> They are singing as they go,
> Marching, marching, to and fro.
> See the soldiers in the street,
> Hear the marching of their feet.

Five Little Monkeys

Mime the actions of each monkey and use your fingers to indicate the number of monkeys as you say this rhyme.

Five little monkeys walked along the shore;
One went a-sailing,
Then there were four.

Four little monkeys climbed up a tree;
One of them tumbled down,
Then there were three.

Three little monkeys found a pot of glue;
One got stuck in it,
Then there were two.

Two little monkeys found a currant bun;
One ran away with it,
Then there was one.

One little monkey cried all afternoon,
So they put him in an airplane
And sent him to the moon.

CHAPTER EIGHT

Early Learning Fun

Before I got married I had six theories about bringing up children. Now I have six children and no theories.
LORD ROCHESTER

THE NAME OF THIS CHAPTER SEEMS TO IMPLY THAT THE ACTIVITIES contained within are the only ones in this book from which your child will learn. In reality, children are learning all the time. Toddlers learn with their hands, their ears, their nose, their mouth, and their feet. They learn by doing: looking, touching, smelling, tasting, banging, dropping, and listening. A toddler's play is her pathway to learning.

In that respect, most of the activities throughout this book provide learning opportunities for toddlers: building with blocks; playing with mud, sand, and water; swinging, sliding, and running outdoors; moving to music; crafting with paper, paints, and glue. All these activities help your child learn and help her make sense of the world around her.

The best way to optimize your child's ability to learn is to create a stimulating environment for her. Provide her with lots of exposure to interesting things to see, touch, and hear. Recite rhymes, sing, and play finger games as you change her diaper (post one or two new rhymes or songs by the changing table to help you learn them). Look through magazines for colourful pictures of everyday objects; paste them onto cardboard, cover with clear contact paper, and display them on the wall by the crib, changing table, or highchair. And most importantly, talk, talk, talk to your child about everything you're doing.

Don't be in a rush to push academics. Young children, toddlers in particular, must spend lots of time developing their motor skills in order to make academic learning possible and productive. Activities that develop large motor skills include running, jumping, hopping, and dancing; and playing with balls, pull toys, push toys, riding toys, climbing toys, swings, and slides. Activities that develop fine motor skills include filling and emptying boxes and containers; and playing with nesting and stacking toys, simple wooden jigsaw puzzles, shape-sorters and blocks. You'll find ideas for these types of activities in various chapters throughout this book.

The activities in this chapter deal primarily with those skills we think of as "academic": sorting, matching, and classifying; and recognizing patterns, shapes, colours, and so on. All these skills are required in order for a child to learn basic math and reading skills. But your toddler can learn these skills any number of ways. For instance, playing with Duplo is a great way to learn basic math skills: sort it by colour, by size, build towers then compare smallest to largest, count the pieces, make patterns, and so on. These are all essential activities for math readiness.

Many of the ideas in this chapter are not for everyone. Some will require a fair amount of time to prepare, making them more suitable to a day-care or preschool setting where more than one child will benefit. If you do choose to spend time assembling these activities, be sure to protect them as best you can. Covering with clear contact paper makes cards and other items more durable. Storage is also important. Shoeboxes and diaper-wipe container are great for storage and they stack nicely on shelves or in cupboards. Smaller sets of cards should be zipped into a Ziploc bag and stored in a large, covered, plastic container along with similar items (for instance, store colour-related activities in one container, shape-related activities in another, and so on).

Picture Box

This takes a bit of time to prepare. Start with just a few pictures and add to your collection as time permits.

> File box or recipe-card holder
> Index cards to fit the file box
> Magazine pictures
> Scissors
> Glue
> Clear contact paper

Cut interesting, colourful pictures of familiar objects from magazines. Glue them onto the index cards and cover with clear contact paper. Place the cards in the file box or recipe-card holder. Your toddler will enjoy looking at the pictures by herself or with you. If you use 4-by-6-inch index cards, they will easily fit into a small (one per page) photo album, an easy item to slip into most diaper bags. Take it with you on a long car ride, talking about each picture as you look at it.

You can maintain your Picture Box as your child grows, adding new pictures and perhaps dividing the pictures into categories such as flowers, animals, people, and so on. Your Picture Box will eventually be a great sorting game, too.

Can You Find Your Knee?

This is a game most of us play informally with our children at one time or another. Very young children often easily point to their eyes, nose, mouth, and ears when asked to do so. Encourage them to identify less common body parts including nostrils, eyelashes, fingernails, lips, throat, wrists, knees, ankles, and so on. This will stimulate the development of memory and vocabulary as well as their ability to recognize parts of the body.

Picture Sort

If the cutting and gluing aspect of preparing this activity will take more time than you have, use two sets of matching stickers instead.

Metal lids from frozen juice cans
Double set of pictures (either photographs or from a magazine)
Glue
Clear contact paper
Magnets (optional)
Plastic container, shoebox, or diaper-wipe container

Cut a double set of pictures of family and friends (or pictures from two identical magazines) into a round shape that will fit the lid of a frozen juice can. Glue the pictures onto the lids and cover with clear contact paper. (You should have two sets of lids exactly the same.) Have your child sort the lids into pairs by matching the two pictures that are the same. If you like, glue magnets to the backs of the lids and make this a refrigerator or cookie-sheet activity.

Store the lids in a plastic container, shoebox, or diaper-wipe container with a slit cut in the top. Your toddler will enjoy dropping the lids into the opening to put the game away.

Pictures, Pictures

If you don't have any old calendars with appropriate pictures on hand, check out bookstores in January when they're selling calendars at big discounts. They're a great source of beautiful, big pictures in many different themes.

> Old calendars with pictures of recognizable objects (dogs, cats, cars, and so on)
> Construction paper
> Scissors
> Glue
> Clear contact paper

Cut out several pictures, mount on construction paper, and cover with clear contact paper. If the pictures are a standard size, you can put them in a three-ring binder, otherwise, store them in a box or file folder. Your child will love to look at the pictures. As she gets older, she'll enjoy mixing them up and sorting them out (all the dogs in one pile, cats in another, and so on).

Pompom Fun

> Pompoms in various sizes and colours

Purchase pompoms in a variety of colours and sizes from a fabric or craft store. For very young children, start with no more than three colours or sizes. Use several sizes of pompoms in one colour and encourage your child to sort them by size. Use one size of pompoms in several colours and ask your child to sort them by colour. Store pompoms in a Ziploc bag when not in use.

Spools of thread also work well for sorting and matching. Use two spools of each colour in at least three different colours.

Animal Sort

Stuffed animals

Gather together all the stuffed animals you can find. Help your toddler sort them by colour or by size (using words like small, smaller, smallest, big, bigger, and biggest). Older children may want to sort them by the type of sound they make (loud, soft), or by their habitat (jungle, forest, farm).

Large and Small

Five or six pairs of objects that are similar in every way except size (adult and child sock, long and short pencil, dinner and lunch plate)

Holding up the two matching items, ask your child which one is smaller. Be sure to use terms such as bigger, smaller, shorter, and longer in your everyday conversation to draw attention to the size of objects around you.

Short and Tall

Paper towel rolls
Scissors
Colourful contact paper or giftwrap (optional)

Cut paper towel rolls into several different sizes. If you like, cover them with colourful contact paper. Encourage your child to stand the rolls up in order from shortest to tallest. Store the rolls in an empty coffee can, shoebox, or diaper-wipe container when not in use.

Spoon Match-Up

Two sets of measuring spoons

Mix up two sets of measuring spoons. Encourage your child to match up two spoons of the same size. Use only one set of spoons and have your child order them from smallest to largest.

More Pompom Fun

Pompoms in various sizes and colours
Clear plastic drinking cups
Permanent marker

Use a permanent marker to make dots on the front of a clear plastic cup. One cup should have one dot, another two dots, the next three dots, and so on. You can mark as many cups as you feel your child is able to match. Give her an assortment of pompoms and show her how to drop the same number of pompoms as dots into the cup. If you like, use beans, large nuts, golf tees, large plastic paper clips, small spools of thread, or other small objects in place of pompoms.

Egg Sort

Even toddlers too young for sort and match activities will have fun playing with these colourful plastic eggs.

12 plastic Easter eggs
Glue gun
Egg carton

Purchase a dozen inexpensive plastic Easter eggs in three to six different colours. Use a glue gun to glue the two parts of each egg together. Encourage your child to sort the eggs by colour. If you like, colour the compartments of an egg carton to match each egg; have your child place the eggs in a compartment of the same colour. Store the eggs in the egg carton when not in use.

Pasta Sort

Dried pasta in two or three (or more) different shapes
Bowl or plastic container

Combine two or three different shapes of dried pasta in a bowl or plastic container. Pick out one piece and ask your toddler to find a piece that matches. If you like, have several small containers on hand and ask your toddler to sort the pasta into the containers. For colourful pasta, dye the pasta beforehand using the Pasta Dye recipe in Appendix A.

Memory

This is a great way to recycle giftwrap. You can also make this a seasonal activity by using giftwrap in holiday patterns, or cutting the cards into shapes such as winter mittens, hearts, or Easter eggs.

Giftwrap in a variety of patterns and colours
Small index cards (3-by-5-inch)
Glue
Scissors
Clear contact paper
Clothespins (optional)

Cut giftwrap into 3-by-5-inch rectangles, making two rectangles from each pattern or colour of paper. Glue each rectangle to the small index cards. Cover both sides of the index card with clear contact paper and trim the edges. Make five to ten pairs of cards (more for older children).

Very young children will enjoy simply handling and looking at the cards. Gradually encourage them to lay the cards out faceup and try to clip the matching pairs together with clothespins. Older toddlers and preschoolers will enjoy playing a game of Memory, where all cards are laid out face down and each player takes a turn trying to turn over a matching pair.

Store the cards in a Ziploc bag. If you use clothespins with this game, store both clothespins and cards in a shoebox or diaper-wipe container when not in use.

Colour Game

Help your child learn her colours and sharpen her listening skills at the same time.

Objects of various colours

Give your child various directions by colour (for example, "Put the red bear on the table," "Pick up the blue car," and "Bring me the yellow book.") You can also do this with actions based on the colour of your child's clothes: "If you are wearing green, you may sit down," or "If you are wearing orange, clap your hands."

Pocket Matching

This is a fun game for toddlers, but takes a fair amount of time to prepare. If you've already prepared the Memory game (page 107), use the cards from the Memory game as the handkerchiefs and use the same giftwrap to make the pockets.

> Giftwrap or fabric in four to six different patterns and colours
> Scissors
> Posterboard, file folder, or large piece of cardboard
> Glue
> Clear contact paper
> Utility knife
> Small index cards or pieces of cardboard, posterboard, or heavy paper

Cut a pocket shape from each piece of fabric or giftwrap. Glue the pockets to a large piece of posterboard, file folder, or cardboard, leaving the top of the pocket open. Cover the pockets and posterboard with clear contact paper, opening the top of the pocket with a utility knife. Cut rectangles out of the fabric or giftwrap that will fit into the pocket (these will be the handkerchiefs). Glue them to small index cards or pieces of cardboard and cover both sides with clear contact paper. Your toddler will have fun matching the handkerchiefs to the pockets. Store the handkerchiefs in an envelope or Ziploc bag attached to the back of the posterboard.

Find the Colour

Tell your child, "I see the colour blue. Can you find it?" As you count down from ten to zero, your child must then run to touch something that includes the colour you have named before you finish counting. If you like, set a kitchen timer for ten (or more) seconds and have your child touch an appropriate object before the timer sounds.

Colour Match

Construction paper
Black marker
Crayons

Give your child a crayon that matches the colour of each piece of construction paper (for very young children, start with only two colours). If you like, use a black marker to write the name of the colour on each sheet of construction paper. Hold up one of the pieces of paper and ask her to pick out the crayon of the same colour, or place the papers and crayons on the table and have her match them up that way. Be sure to use the colour names as you do this (for example, "I have a red piece of paper. Can you find the red crayon that will match my paper?").

Colour Cards

Construction paper
Black marker
Scissors
Clear contact paper

Make up two sets of cards from construction paper. Start with only a few colours, working your way up to the nine basic colours (red, green, blue, brown, yellow, orange, purple, black, and white). If you like, write the names of each colour on the card. Cover the cards with clear contact paper. Spread the cards out on a table and begin by picking up one of the cards and saying, "I have a red card. Can you hand me the other red card?" After awhile, your child will enjoy matching the cards all by herself. Store the cards in a small Ziploc bag when not in use.

Cars and Colours

Toy cars
Construction paper

Start with two cars in two different colours, such as red and blue. Have construction paper in red and blue, too. Play with the cars for awhile, then "park" each car on the construction paper of the same colour. Be sure to talk about the cars and their colours as you play. Play with the cars some more, then see if your child can park each car on the matching paper. Add another colour as each is mastered.

Clothespin Colours

Spring-type clothespins
Paint (optional)
Coloured dot stickers (or use white and colour them yourself)
Empty coffee can

Paint five or six clothespins in different colours to match the coloured dot stickers, or decorate each clothespin with additional coloured dot stickers. Stick coloured dot stickers evenly around the top of the coffee can, leaving some space in between. Show your toddler how to clip each clothespin just above the matching coloured dot. Store the clothespins inside the coffee can when not in use.

Colourful Clothespins

Craft-type clothespins (without a spring)
Three empty coffee cans
Paint, crayons, or markers
Construction paper or coloured contact paper

Paint or colour five or six clothespins in the primary colours (red, yellow, and blue). Cover each coffee can with a different primary colour, using construction paper or coloured contact paper. Encourage your older toddler to match the colours as they place the clothespins around the rim of the can. You can also cut a small hole in the plastic lid of the can and have her drop the clothespins through the lid. Store the clothespins in the covered coffee cans when not in use.

Colour Hunt

Help your toddler learn her colours by going on a colour hunt together.

Paper or plastic bags
Hunting hats (optional)

Begin your colour hunt by putting on your hunting hats and picking a colour to hunt. To begin, show your child an object that represents the colour you're looking for, name the colour, then put it in the bag. Do this two or three times, then let your child be the "hunter." When you're finished, empty your bags and name the items together (red sock, red ball, red cup). You can also hunt for colours (without collecting them) at the grocery store or when you're driving along together.

Search and Sort

Make sure the stones you use for this activity are large enough not to pose a choking hazard.

Forty-eight stones (plus a few extras for those that will get lost)
Four empty egg cartons
Paint or spray paint in four different colours
Clear acrylic spray (optional)

Paint twelve stones per colour and let dry; if using tempera paint, you may want to finish with a clear acrylic spray. If you like, paint each of the egg cartons a different colour. Give your child the stones and the egg cartons. She will have fun sorting the stones and storing them in the egg cartons. You can also hide the stones in her sandbox for her to dig up and collect in a bucket.

Parking Game

This simple matching game is lots of fun. Even toddlers with no concept of colour will enjoy parking the cars in the garages, whether they match or not.

> Small boxes (shoeboxes work well, as do some cereal boxes)
> Three or four toy cars in different colours
> Scissors
> Construction paper
> Glue
> Paint or coloured contact paper (optional)

In one side of each box cut a garage door big enough to fit a toy car. Cover each box with coloured construction paper, matching the colours of the paper to the cars. (If you like, use coloured contact paper or paint the boxes instead.) Turn each box upside down so the bottom of the box is the roof of the garage. Encourage your child to park each car in the garage of the same colour. Store the garages and cars in a larger box or plastic container when not in use.

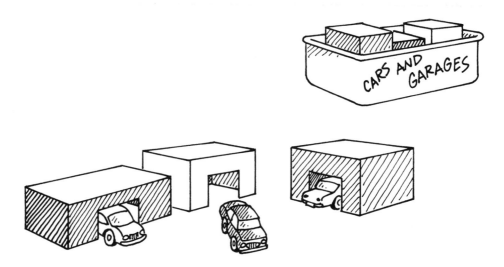

Colour Cube

This cube is made in the same way as Toddler Blocks in Chapter 2. Use the illustration on page 44 to help you make this cube.

> Empty milk cartons (any size will do)
> Tape
> Construction or contact paper in six different colours
> Scissors
> Glue
> Clear contact paper

Choose two milk cartons the same size. For each carton, measure the base and make a cutting line that same distance up the side of the carton. Cut along the lines on both cartons. You should now have two open-ended cubes. Push one cube into the other so that all sides are closed. Tape around the cut edges.

Cut squares to fit one side of the cube out of six different colours of construction paper. Glue one square to each face of the cube. Cover with clear contact paper for durability.

You can use your colour cube in many different ways:

▲ Have your child throw the cube up in the air; when it lands, ask her to bring you something that matches the colour on top of the cube.

◀ Cut squares of construction paper in the same colours as the cube and cover with clear contact paper. When she tosses the cube in the air, have her hand you the colour card that matches the colour on top of the cube.

▶ Match the colours on the colour cube to crayons, toys, or Duplo.

◀ Use your imagination and come up with some ideas of your own. You can also make a shape cube and matching set of shape cards and play in the same way.

Mailman

> Construction paper
> Scissors
> Shoeboxes or plastic baskets
> Clear contact paper

Cut circles, squares, and triangles out of various colours of construction paper. Cover the shapes with clear contact paper. Tape one of each shape (if sorting by shapes) or each colour (if sorting by colours) to a shoebox or small plastic basket. Give the remaining shapes to your child and have her play Mailman—delivering all the shapes or colours to their proper mailbox. You can also play this game with Duplo, wooden blocks, or other items you may have around the house. Try varying the classification, sorting by big and small, hard and soft, and so on.

If using baskets, they will stack nicely in a cupboard or on a shelf when not in use. Store the cards in a Ziploc bag with the baskets.

Turntable Fun

Double set of stickers, shapes, or colours
Glue
Scissors
Construction paper
Clear contact paper
Plastic kitchen turntable

Use a double set of stickers, or cut a double set of simple shapes or colours from construction paper. If using stickers, stick one set of stickers on small squares of construction paper. Cover the construction paper with clear contact paper. Stick the other set of stickers, shapes, or colours around the outer edge of a plastic kitchen turntable. Slowly move the turntable and have your child match the shapes, colours, or stickers in her hand with the ones on the turntable. If matching colours, try matching a crayon to the colour on the turntable.

Beanbag Toss

Large sheet of paper
Markers or paints
Beanbag

On a large sheet of paper, draw or paint several large shapes in different colours (or cut shapes out of construction paper and lay them on the floor). Have your child stand a few feet away and toss a beanbag onto the shapes. Have her identify the colour and/or shape the beanbag landed on. As she becomes more skilled, ask her to aim for a certain shape (for example, "Let's try for the red square this time. Oops! You hit the yellow circle!").

Shape Match-Up

Construction paper in four different colours
Scissors
Clear contact paper

Cut out two sets of the four basic geometric shapes (circle, triangle, square, rectangle) from construction paper, using a different colour for each shape. Cover with clear contact paper. Give one set to your child. Hold up one shape from your set and ask her if she can find the matching shape from her set, being sure to call the shape by its name as you do ("I have a circle. Can you find a circle, too?"). You can also mix up both sets on the table and have your child pick out the matching shapes. If you think your child is matching by colour, or by associating a certain shape with a certain colour, try it again with a new set of shapes in different colours, or make the shapes all the same colour. Store the shapes in a Ziploc bag when not in use.

Alphabet Sand

Sand, salt, or sugar
Metal pie plate

Pour sand, salt, or sugar into a metal pie plate. Your child can learn her letters by making their shapes with her index finger in the sand. Start with simple letters like O, C, V, or X. Avoid salt if your child has a cut on her finger; avoid sugar if you think she may eat more than she spells!

Object Match-Up

> Paper
> Household objects
> Pencil, pen, or marker
> Clear contact paper
> Scissors
> Box or bag

Gather several common household objects, such as a spoon, cookie cutter, or key (something with a recognizable shape). Place each object on a separate piece of paper and trace around its shape. Cover the sheets of paper with clear contact paper. Put all the objects inside a box or bag and spread the pages with the outlined shapes on the table or floor. Have your child remove an object from the box or bag and match it to its outline.

Store the objects and their outlines in a shoebox or diaper-wipe container when not in use.

Tape Shapes

> Masking tape or colourful tape

Use masking tape or colourful tape to make several different shapes on the floor. Call out different movements, such as "Crawl to the square," "Hop to the circle," or "Run to the triangle."

If you like, make a Shape Cube (see Colour Cube, this chapter) with the same shapes on it as you have taped on the floor. Throw the Shape Cube into the air and, when it lands, have your child move to the same shape as is displayed on the top of the cube.

Find Mr. Different

    Regular-sized paper, cut in half vertically
    Markers, shapes cut out of construction paper, or stickers
    Clear contact paper
    Scissors

On each strip of paper make a set of pictures or symbols that are all the same except for one (for example, five happy faces, one sad face; five cat stickers, one dog sticker; five triangles, one circle; and so on). Cover with clear contact paper. Ask your child to find Mr. Different. Older children can explain how he differs from the others in the set.

    Store the strips in a large Ziploc bag when not in use.

Practical Math

Give your child the opportunity to develop math skills in her everyday world. Count everything with your child: steps as you climb them, toys as you pick them up, cups as you set the table. Take your child on household counting assignments (for example, count the number of doors in your house, including closets). Count out loud with your child as you match napkins to place mats, forks to spoons, and so on.

Paper Plate Numbers

Twenty small paper plates
Black marker
Stickers or dots

Make up a matching set of paper plates with numbers from one to ten. Put one sticker around the edge of each of two plates, and write the numeral and/or word "1" in the centre of the plate. Make up a pair with the rest of the numerals to ten in the same way. You can use this as a hands-on matching activity, or just display the plates on a wall in her bedroom or wherever your child spends time during the day.

Playdough Numbers

Construction paper, or white or coloured paper
Marker
Clear contact paper
Playdough

Use a broad-tip marker to write the numerals 0 to 10, using one piece of paper for each numeral. Cover each piece of paper with clear contact paper. Show your child how to roll playdough into "ropes," and shape the playdough on each piece of paper to match the shape of the numeral.

Number Cube

This cube is made in the same way as Toddler Blocks in Chapter 2. If you like, look at the illustration on page 44 to help you make this cube.

Empty milk cartons (any size will do)
Tape
Construction paper
Clear contact paper
Scissors
Permanent marker
Six small objects for counting (pompoms, beans, large nuts, golf tees, large plastic paper clips)

Choose two milk cartons the same size. For each carton, measure the base and make a cutting line that same distance up the side of the carton. Cut along the lines on both cartons. You should now have two open-ended cubes. Push one cube into the other so that all sides are closed. Tape around the cut edges.

Wrap the entire cube in a sheet of paper. On each face of the cube use a permanent marker to make a different number of dots (or use dot stickers) from one to six. Cover the cube in clear contact paper.

Give your child six small objects to count with. Show her how to throw the die in the air and count out the same number of objects as dots on the top of the cube. If you like, substitute raisins, small pieces of cereal, or chocolate chips for the objects to count with. Count out the correct number, then eat them!

Sock Match-Up

This will help your child match up her socks and learn her numbers at the same time.

> Permanent laundry marker
> Socks

Number each pair of your child's socks with a permanent laundry marker. You can have her match up her socks as you fold the laundry, or place them in her drawer and have her match them as she wears them.

Apple Seed Count

> Apple
> Knife
> Paint (optional)
> Paper (optional)

Cut an apple in half and remove all the apple seeds. Count the seeds with your child. Eat the apple for a snack or dip it in paint and press onto paper to make an apple print.

CHAPTER NINE

Music and Movement

The commonest fallacy among women is that simply having children makes one a mother—which is as absurd as believing that having a piano makes one a musician.
SYDNEY J. HARRIS

ANYONE WHO HAS EVER WATCHED A BABY'S REACTION TO MUSIC KNOWS that babies seem to be born with a sense of music and rhythm. Even before they're old enough to walk, many will bob their heads and wiggle their little bodies when lively music comes on. Once they can walk, just try to stop them from jiggling and dancing anytime, anywhere they hear a snappy beat.

Often the first music your child hears will come from you. Don't worry if you can't carry a tune; your voice is the most beautiful one he hears. Sing as you rock him, walk him, carry him, change him, bathe him, and play with him. If you don't know many songs, borrow a few tapes or CDs of children's songs from the library, or buy them for your own collection.

Children also seem to have a natural instinct for movement. Once he can walk, run, jump, and climb, there are many days when it seems that is all he wants to do. Movement activities are important as they help your child develop his large motor skills. Moving to music is equally important as it helps your child experience movement as it relates to music or rhythm.

Listening to, moving to, and making music should be part of every day for you and your child. These activities have many benefits, but for most children they are just plain fun!

Coffee Can Drum

Empty coffee can with two plastic lids
Contact paper or your child's artwork
Glue
Pencil
Empty thread spool

You can create a drum for your child by cutting the bottom out of a coffee can and covering the can with contact paper (or let your child draw a picture on some paper and glue around the can). Glue plastic lids on each end of the can. Create a drumstick by gluing the lead end of a pencil into the hole of an empty thread spool.

For a variation, an empty paper towel roll and an empty oatmeal box will make a soft but authentic drum for your toddler.

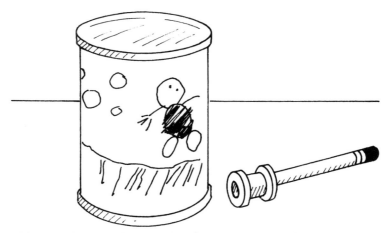

Button Tap

Large buttons with two holes
Rubber bands
Empty cooking pots
Small glove, needle, and thread (optional)

Insert the looped ends of a rubber band into the two holes of a large button. Bring the looped ends together and slide onto your child's finger. Put a few of these on each hand and let your child tap out some music on an upside-down pot.

For a variation, sew small buttons onto the fingers of a small glove. Place the glove on your child's hand and let him tap around the house.

Strumming Fun

> Corrugated cardboard
> Spoon

Show your child how to strum a spoon along the rippled edge of a piece of corrugated cardboard for a neat sound.

Kazoo

> Empty toilet paper roll
> Thin paper (newspaper works well)
> White glue
> Hole punch
> Scissors

Punch a hole in the side of the empty toilet paper roll as far from the end as the punch will reach. Cut a square of paper large enough to cover one end of the roll. Coat the edge of the roll with glue and place it firmly down onto the square of paper. Leave the roll standing on the paper until the glue is completely dry. If you like, your child can decorate his kazoo with crayons, markers, or stickers.

To play the kazoo, show your child how to put his mouth against the open end of the kazoo and hum.

Paper Bag Shaker

Paper bag
Rice or dried beans
Ribbon or rubber band

Make a simple shaker for your toddler by putting a small amount of rice or dried beans into a paper bag (you may want to decorate the bag with markers or stickers first). Tie the bag securely with a piece of ribbon or a rubber band. This simple shaker can add a lot of enjoyment to your songs and dance.

Simple Shaker

Empty film canisters or small plastic bottles
Small rocks, beads, buttons, popping corn
Glue

Place a few rocks, beads, buttons, pieces of popping corn, or other small objects into an empty film canister or other small plastic container. Glue the lid on securely to prevent a possible choking hazard.

Toddler Triangle

Two large (5-inch) nails
Masking tape
String

Cover the sharp ends of the nails with tape. Tie a string around the head of one of the large nails. While holding onto the string, tap the "triangle" with the "striker" (the other nail).

Tiny Tambourine

Two small aluminum tart pans (about 3-inch diameter)
Dried beans, corn, pennies, and so on
Stapler or tape

Put a handful of dried beans, corn, or pennies in a small aluminum tart pan. Place another tart pan over the top of the first and staple or tape the edges together.

Jingle Bell Bracelet

You might think this most appropriate as a Christmas activity, but toddlers will enjoy jingling any time of the year.

Jingle bells
Elastic
Scissors

Cut the elastic long enough to fit your child's wrist and add a few inches for tying. String three or four jingle bells onto the elastic and tie the ends together. Slip the bracelet onto your child's wrist or ankle, put some music on, and listen to the bells jingle as he dances or claps around the house.

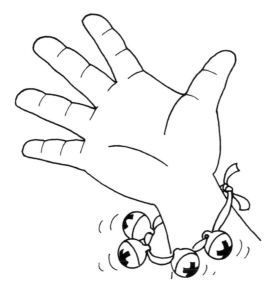

Jingle Bell Roller

Empty coffee can with lid
Jingle bells or jar lids

Put bells or metal jar lids inside the empty coffee can. Securely glue or tape the plastic lid onto the coffee can. Your child can help you decorate the outside of the coffee can. If you like, glue a piece of contact paper sticky side out around the can, then have your toddler stick on pictures cut from magazines, pieces of giftwrap, or whatever you have on hand. Cover with another piece of contact paper. Your child will have fun shaking this or rolling it across the floor.

Easter Egg Maracas

Small, plastic Easter eggs
Pennies, dried beans, small rocks, popping corn, beads, buttons, and
  so on
Glue gun
Empty egg carton

Gather together a variety of items to fill the plastic Easter eggs. Try pennies, dried beans, small rocks, popping corn, beads, buttons, and so on. Fill each egg with a different substance and firmly glue the two pieces of the egg together. Store in an egg carton. Toddlers will enjoy taking the eggs in and out of the carton as well as shaking them to hear the different sounds they make.

For older children, fill two eggs with each substance. Have them shake the eggs and match up the pairs by listening to the sounds they make.

Dance Ribbon

Empty key chain or plastic shower curtain ring
Long lengths of brightly coloured ribbon or plastic

Attach 3- or 4-foot lengths of brightly coloured ribbon or plastic to an empty key chain or plastic shower curtain ring. Your child can wave the ribbon in the air as he runs, or twirl it in time to the music as he dances.

Dancing with Scarves

Scarves are a versatile item to have on hand for toddlers. Lightweight, chiffon-type scarves are great for dancing with.

Scarf
Music

Choose a light, breezy type of scarf for your child to dance with. If the scarf is too long, tie a knot in the middle to form a handle. Encourage your child to wave his scarf in the air in time to the music.

Dance and Fall Down

Music

Put on some music and dance around the room with your child. When the music stops, everyone falls down. When the music begins again, everyone gets up and dances some more.

Stop!

Face your child and hold his hands. Walk slowly in a circle and sing or recite this poem as you walk:

Round and round and round we go,
Round and round and round we go,
Round and round and round we go.
Round and round and STOP!

Freeze when you say "STOP!" Repeat the game as many times as your child wants to, changing directions and speeding up a little each time.

Row, Row, Row Your Boat

Sit on the floor across from your child, legs spread far enough apart so that you can hold hands. Pull your child towards you, then lean forward and have your child lean back. Continue the rocking motion, forward and back, as you sing the familiar song "Row, Row, Row Your Boat" or other rocking rhymes.

Follow the Leader

Young children are such a bundle of energy. A short "exercise class" not only helps with their large muscle development, but it can be a sanity saver on a long, rainy day indoors. You'll feel better afterwards, too! Encourage your child to follow your lead as you exercise together. Try touching toes, running in place, swinging your arms, and stretching to the ceiling. Exercise to music, pass a ball back and forth, or twirl a long ribbon in the air. For a change, let your child be the leader and you follow his example.

Let's Pretend

This activity will give your child's large muscles a workout along with his imagination. Give your child a series of instructions such as, "Let's pretend you are a rabbit. Can you hop like a rabbit?" or, "Let's pretend you are an elephant. Can you walk about like a big, heavy elephant?" Try other animals, plants growing in the ground, a flower opening on a summer day, or a balloon being filled with air.

Climbing Practice

> Couch cushions or large pillows

Make a big, soft pile of couch cushions or large pillows on the floor. Your toddler will have fun climbing and rolling around on them. For older toddlers, stack the cushions up like stairs against the couch and let him practice climbing up and down.

Toddler Trampoline

> Crib mattress
> Crib sheet
> Pillows

Place a crib mattress on the floor, away from any dangerous edges or corners. Cover the mattress with a crib sheet and surround it with pillows for safety. Your child will enjoy jumping and bouncing on his toddler-sized trampoline.

Mirror Play

This activity will probably be best enjoyed by one-year-olds.

Large mirror

Stand or sit with your child in front of a large mirror. Ask your child what he sees, and point out his head, arms, legs, feet, and so on. Encourage him to make movements and watch what happens to his reflection as he does. Put on some music and watch him move and dance in time to the beat. You may want to have your camera on hand in case he tries to kiss his reflection.

Toddler Gymnastics

Simple gymnastics will not only burn up some of your toddler's seemingly endless energy, but will also encourage his eye-body coordination, necessary for balance and depth perception. Encourage your toddler in simple gymnastics such as tumbling, rolling, climbing, and sliding. If you like, put on some snappy music or play "Follow the Leader." Show your child the basic movements then take turns being the leader.

▲ CHAPTER TEN ▲
Arts and Crafts

It would seem that something which means poverty, disorder, and violence every single day should be avoided entirely, but the desire to beget children is a natural urge.   PHYLLIS DILLER

ART AND CRAFT ACTIVITIES PROVIDE MANY VALUABLE LEARNING experiences for toddlers. Your child will begin to learn to think creatively, and activities such as drawing, painting, cutting, pasting, and playing with playdough and other craft materials help develop her small motor and manipulative skills.

One important thing to keep in mind when doing any art or craft activity with a young child is that it's the process—not the product—that counts. By this I mean that activities which can provide so much benefit to a toddler can also lead to frustration and disappointment for both adult and child if the parent or other caregiver comes to the activity with a final product in mind. The adult who has an expected outcome from a toddler art or craft activity will, out of necessity, do a lot of the work for the child. The child will end up with a nice picture or object, but any skills she may have developed from that experience will be lost or minimized. Even something as simple as using a glue stick is important for little ones, so resist the urge to grab it out of your child's hands and do it yourself if she's not doing it "right." We all know it would look better and go faster and be neater if we did it for them, but if they're to gain any benefit at all from the activity, they have to do the work themselves.

Karen Miller, in her book *More Things to Do With Toddlers and Twos* (Telshare Publishing Co. Ltd., Chelsea, MA, 1990), lists five general principles for doing art with toddlers. While she is writing primarily for teachers of toddlers, these are great guidelines to keep in mind whether you are working with many toddlers or just one.

1. Don't tell your child what to make, and don't expect her final product to be recognizable. Telling a two-year-old to make a mailbox or an Easter basket only sets them up for failure, as she cannot possibly do it herself. Instead, Miller says, "value the basic scribble." The most important thing for your child is the experience of freely exploring art and craft materials. Toddlers simply cannot control the materials well enough to make a representational drawing.

2. Focus on providing interesting materials. Toddlers are basically interested in cause and effect, whether they are playing with water, building with blocks, or working on an art project such as finger-painting, pasting, or painting with a brush. Your goal in providing your toddler with art experiences should be to expose her to as many different materials and processes as possible. Let her play with warm playdough one day, cold the next; mix paint thick one time, thin another; use wide and narrow paintbrushes as well as sponges, cotton swabs, and feathers for painting.

3. Let the child do the whole project. The activity only has value for the child if she does it herself. In making a collage with glue, the value for the child comes in spreading the glue on the page, noticing how it feels on her fingers, and so on. If you spread the glue on and then provide the items for your child to stick to the page, much of the value of the activity is lost.

4. Do art with one child at a time, or very small groups. Art projects with toddlers should be undertaken on a one-on-one basis. Miller says that "with your undivided attention, the child can really concentrate on the material in front of her and enjoy seeing what she can do with it." If you do have other young children to care for, have other interesting things prepared for them to do while you're working one-on-one, or allow them to stand around and watch if they want to. Older two- and three-year-olds may enjoy doing art in groups of three or four.

5. Allow children to repeat experiences. Sometimes we may feel that providing our children with a variety of experiences means never doing the same thing twice. What we're really doing, however, is

not allowing our child to fully explore an activity, meaning that the child cannot learn or develop as much. Allowing your toddler to repeat an activity several times gives her the opportunity to fully explore it and, as Miller states, "encourages the development of concentration and experimentation, both elements of creativity."

Don't forget to display the artwork your child has created. Post it on walls, doors, and of course the refrigerator. Use it to create a custom tablecloth: cover your table with a plain, dark tablecloth, arrange your child's artwork on it, then cover with a clear, vinyl tablecloth. Use your child's artwork as a gift or giftwrap when possible. If you like, create a portfolio for your child. Use a 3-ring binder and plastic page protectors to save some of your child's earliest or most outstanding creations (be sure to date or write your child's age on each work of art). For extra large or three-dimensional projects that can't be saved permanently, take a photo or two and put those in the binder.

The activities in this chapter will help you provide your toddler with a variety of art and craft experiences. These experiences should be fun for you and your child, so don't undertake painting or other messy projects when you're tired, rushed, or otherwise unable to devote yourself fully to what your toddler is doing. If approached with the right attitude, you and your toddler will have a wonderful time of creating, exploring, and discovering the world of art.

SCRIBBLING AND DRAWING

When I first became a mother, I purchased a very good book on things to do with babies. It stated that children should start to scribble between nine and twelve months of age, and it even outlined the procedure to follow: seat your child comfortably, then give her some paper and a big, fat crayon. Show her how to make marks on the page, then watch her go!

I was horrified to realize that time had gotten away on me! My daughter, already past her first birthday, had not yet had her first experience with crayons and paper. After a quick run to the store, I optimistically seated her in her highchair, taped down a blank piece of paper, showed her how to hold the crayon, and let her go to it. You can imagine my dismay when she began eating the crayon and tearing the paper! She wasn't lagging behind developmentally, as I initially feared. She just wasn't ready for the whole scribbling experience.

When ready for it, most toddlers will find scribbling a lot of fun. It allows them to experiment with cause and effect while developing small muscles and hand-eye coordination. Cynthia Catlin, in her book *Toddlers Together: The Complete Planning Guide for a Toddler Curriculum* (Gryphon House, Beltsville, MD, 1994) says, "Scribbling is the precursor to writing, just as babbling is to talking. A better term for scribbling would be M.I.M.s, for these are the Most Important Marks a toddler can make."

Provide your toddler with a variety of drawing tools and materials: crayons, markers, pens, pencil crayons, and chalk. For drawing paper, use construction paper, newspaper, fine sandpaper, or cut-open grocery bags. Remember to include three-dimensional surfaces such as boxes and rocks.

If replacing caps on markers is a problem, make this simple marker holder: Mix plaster of Paris in a small plastic container that is at least as deep as a marker top. Set the marker tops in the wet plaster with the open end up. Be sure that the plaster does not cover the open end of the marker top. When the plaster dries, press the markers into their tops that have dried into the plaster. Remind your child to stand the markers back in the marker holder when she has finished using them.

Rainbow Crayons

This idea appears in *Surviving Your Preschooler,* but it's worth repeating here. These crayons are beautiful, and easy for little hands to hold!

> Broken crayon pieces
> Clean, empty tin cans
> Pot of hot water
> Empty, plastic 35-mm film canisters

This is a great way to use broken crayons. Remove any paper from the crayons and sort them by colour. Place the pieces, one colour at a time, in the empty tin cans. Set the tin cans in a pot of very hot or boiling water until the crayons have melted. Pour a small amount (approximately a quarter inch) into each film canister. When the wax hardens, add a second colour in the same way. When you're done, you will have a crayon rainbow of layered colours.

Foot Tracing

Drawing paper
Crayons, markers, or paints

Have your child stand on a piece of paper while you trace around her feet with a pen or crayon. Then trace your own feet and compare sizes. Colour the feet with crayons, markers, or paints. Older children may want to use crayons, markers, or paint to add nail polish and funny rings to the toes.

Marker Drawing

A good way to get more use out of dried-up markers.

Dried-up markers
Water
Paper

Let your child dip dried-up markers in water and use them like water-colours on paper. When the tip turns white, you can throw them away or dip them in paint and write or draw on paper.

Chalk Fun

There was a time that chalk was just for chalkboards and sidewalks. Now, inexpensive chalk is available in a variety of colours and thicknesses, and you can use it creatively in many different art endeavours. The following ideas will help you use chalk in ways you may not have considered or known about before.

Chalk
Paper
Hair spray (optional)
Water (optional)
Sponge (optional)
Liquid starch (optional)
Buttermilk (optional)
Paintbrush (optional)
Sugar (optional)
Cotton balls (optional)

▲ Draw with chalk on a piece of plain or construction paper. Spray with hair spray to set the chalk.

◀ Wet your paper with a damp sponge and draw on the wet paper with chalk.

▶ Paint a piece of paper with liquid starch; while wet, make designs with coloured chalk.

◀ Brush buttermilk over the surface of your paper, then use chalk to draw on it.

▼ Place a piece of paper on a textured surface (like a sidewalk) or over a greeting card with a raised design. Rub a piece of chalk sideways over the paper to make a chalk rubbing of the texture or design.

▶ Soak chalk in water, then draw on a window with the wet chalk. It will easily wash away when you're done.

◀ Soak chalk in a mixture of one cup water and one-third cup sugar for five to ten minutes. Draw with the wet chalk on a piece of paper. Use a cotton ball to smudge the chalk marks on the paper.

▼ Draw on a wet sponge with chalk. Press the sponge onto a piece of plain or construction paper to make a print of the design.

Cylinder Pictures

Paper
Markers or crayons
Tape

Have your child draw on a rectangular piece of paper. When she's done, roll the paper into a cylinder and tape the ends together. Set it on a shelf or mantle for all to admire.

Toddler Mural

Large sheet of drawing paper
Art easel (optional)
Fat, "toddler" crayons
Yarn
Scissors

Tape a large sheet of drawing paper to the easel. Cut several pieces of yarn about two feet in length. Cut a small notch at one end of each crayon and wrap and tie a length of yarn around it. Tie the other end of the yarn to the top of the easel. (Be sure to cut the yarn long enough to reach the paper, but not so long that it would be a choking hazard.) Now your toddler can come and scribble any time she wants without waiting for you to set out the crayons and paper.

If you don't have an art easel, use an old wall in the basement or playroom instead. Tape a large sheet of paper to the wall. Above the paper, hammer in a few nails and attach the yarn and crayons to the nails.

Paper Towel Drawing

A quick and easy activity for even the youngest toddlers.

Paper towel or coffee filters
Markers

Set your toddler in her highchair and give her a couple of markers and a coffee filter or piece of paper towel. The absorbency of the paper towel will make the colours blur as she makes marks on it.

PAINTING

A child's love for paint begins at an early age and lasts for many years, if not a lifetime. A clean sheet of paper before her, pots of paint in vivid colours, big paintbrushes to wield as she wills—what could make a toddler happier?

If proper preparations have been made, this art experience can be enjoyed by the parent or caregiver, too. Before you begin a painting session with your toddler, consider the following guidelines:

▲ Don't undertake a painting session with your toddler when you're tired, rushed, or otherwise unable to devote yourself fully to what your child is doing.

▼ Cover up the work space appropriately. I cover the kitchen table with an old sheet that I throw in the wash when the painting session is over.

▶ If you don't have a painter's smock or large, old t-shirt to cover your child, dress her in old clothes that you can afford to set aside as painting clothes (even washable paints may not wash out completely).

◀ Add a little dish detergent or water and soap flakes to the paint. It makes cleanup easier.

The best kind of paint for young children is poster paint, also known as tempera paint. You can buy this at any art store in premixed liquid form or as a powder that must be mixed with water. You can also make your own poster paint using the recipes in Appendix A. Children rarely need more than three colours: red, blue, and yellow. Teach your child how to mix these colours to create others. Tempera blocks are also available. They're practical because they don't have to be diluted and they can't be spilled, making cleanup easier. In addition, tempera blocks are economical and last a long time.

However, your child will probably not find them as fun as slick liquid paints. Empty baby food jars work well as paint jars. You can use a sponge to prevent the jar from tipping; the sponge will also soak up any drips. Simply cut a hole in the sponge the size of the jar and fit the jar into the sponge. You can also make a simple toddler-sized paint palette by gluing plastic milk lids to a piece of heavy cardboard. Pour a small amount of paint into each lid. For a more permanent palette, nail several baby food jar lids to a block of wood.

Paper can be purchased from an art supply store, but consider some of the following alternatives. Newsprint is a wonderful paper for painting, and roll-ends can be purchased cheaply from a newspaper publisher. Visit your local printer and ask if you can leave an empty box for a week or two. She may agree to fill it with all kinds of wonderful paper that would otherwise be discarded. Also try fine sandpaper as an alternative art paper for a wonderful effect. For fingerpainting, use the shiny side of freezer paper that can be purchased at the grocery store. It's much cheaper than special fingerpaint paper and works just as well.

If you have an old wall you don't care about too much, cover it with a large piece of contact paper. You can tape the painting paper directly to the contact paper, and it will wipe up easily. The contact paper will likely damage the wall if you try to remove it, so be careful where you put it.

A tabletop easel can be made by removing one side of a cardboard box and taping the remaining three sides to form a triangle shape. Tape one side to the table and attach a piece of paper to one of the other sides. Use it for painting or drawing.

Here are a few more tips to keep in mind when working with paint:

- ▲ Water and soap flakes or detergent added to paint make it easier to wash out.
- ◀ Liquid detergent added to paint will help prevent cracking.
- ▶ Liquid starch will make the paint thicker.
- ▼ Powdered alum can be used as a preservative.
- ▶ Salt, crushed egg shells, and coffee grounds give paint an interesting texture.

◀ Condensed milk will give paint a glossier finish.

◀ Baby powder mixed with tempera paint will extend the paint and add a nice smell.

▼ Plastic cafeteria trays are ideal for toddlers to paint on, with or without paper.

▲ String up a line in the laundry room or kitchen that can be used to hang paintings to dry. Wet artwork can be attached to the line with clothespins.

When dry, be sure to display your child's paintings prominently. And think of creative uses for some of her work—many painting projects make wonderful giftwrap or greeting cards.

Sheet Painting

Spray bottle
Water
Liquid tempera paint
Old sheet

Fill a spray bottle half-and-half with water and tempera paint. For some creative outdoor fun, hang an old sheet on a fence or clothesline and have your child spray paint it.

Straw Painting

If your child has mastered the skill of blowing, she may enjoy this activity. If not, she will still enjoy using the straw like a paintbrush.

> Tempera paint
> Paper
> Drinking straw

Drop a bit of thin paint on a piece of paper. Give your child a straw and have her blow the paint around. If you like, add a second and third colour. You can also use different types of paper for different effects.

Food Colouring Painting

> Food colouring
> Water
> Paintbrush
> Paper towel or coffee filter

Add food colouring to water, enough to achieve the colour you want. Brush the food colouring and water mixture onto a piece of paper towel or coffee filter. Use several colours. When the paper towel is soaked, remove and let dry, then mount on construction paper to display.

Fly Swatter Painting

This is definitely an outdoor activity. If this is just "something to do," then one colour of paint is enough. For a nicer looking painting, try using two or three colours of paint, one after the other.

> Fly swatter
> Paint
> Baking pan or cookie sheet
> Large sheets of paper

Put up large sheets of paper outside, either by taping them to a fence or clipping them to a clothesline. Pour paint into the baking pan or cookie sheet. Show your child how to dip the fly swatter into the paint and slap it onto the paper.

Marker Painting

Dried-up markers
Tempera paint
Paper

Let your child use dried-up markers in place of a paintbrush. Dip them in liquid tempera paint and use to write or draw on paper.

Dry Painting

For a painting activity, this is pretty clean and requires little preparation.

Cotton balls
Clothespins (spring-type)
Powdered tempera paint
Paper
Hair spray

Clip a cotton ball onto the end of a spring-type clothespin. Sprinkle a few colours of powdered tempera paint onto a piece of paper. Show your toddler how to use the cotton ball to spread the paint around the paper. When the painting is done, spray with hair spray to set the paint. This makes a nice greeting card.

Crumple Painting

Here's another easy way for your young child to make wrapping paper.

> Liquid tempera paint or soap paint (see Frosty Snow Painting)
> Newspaper
> Heavy plain paper

Crumple up some newspaper into a ball and dip it in liquid tempera or soap paint. Press the newspaper ball lightly all over the heavy plain paper. Use two or three different colours if you like. Let dry.

Paint with Water

> Black marker
> Paper towel
> Paintbrush
> Water

Draw a picture or shape with a thick, black marker on a piece of paper towel. Show your child how to brush water over the marker lines and watch how the colours seep out.

Ice Popsicle Painting

This variation of Paint Popsicles is more suited to younger children. If you think your child may lick the ice Popsicle after it's been painted with, substitute Kool-Aid drink mix or jelly powder crystals for powdered paint.

> Water
> Popsicle mould
> Powdered tempera paint
> Paper

Freeze water in a Popsicle mould to make ice Popsicles. Remove from the freezer a few minutes before using to allow the ice to melt a little. Sprinkle a little tempera powder on a piece of paper. Your child can paint by rubbing the ice Popsicle over the paint on the paper. For variety, use Kool-Aid drink mix or Jell-O jelly powder in place of the powdered tempera paint.

Paint Popsicles

Please supervise this activity carefully and use it only with children who are not likely to lick these Popsicles. For safer variations for really young children, try Ice Popsicle Painting or Ice Cube Painting.

> Liquid tempera paint
> Water
> Popsicle mould
> Paper

Mix liquid tempera paint with water (half-and-half) and pour into a Popsicle mould. Insert sticks and place in the freezer until frozen. Remove paint Popsicles from the freezer about ten minutes before you want to use them. Give your child the paint Popsicle and a large piece of paper and let her paint away.

Ice Cube Painting

> Ice cubes
> Paper
> Powdered tempera paint
> Flat box (the kind a 24-pack of pop comes in) or large baking pan

Place a sheet of paper in the box or baking pan. Sprinkle a little tempera powder on the paper. Place the ice cube in the box and let your child rotate the box around to make a pretty painting. If you like, substitute Kool-Aid drink mix or Jell-O jelly powder for the powdered tempera paint.

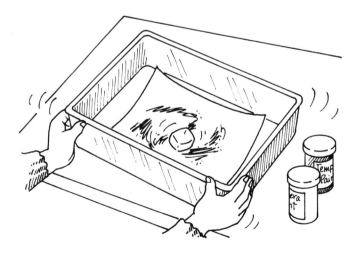

Magic Painting

"Paint with water" book
Ice cube or ice Popsicle

For a variation on painting with a brush and water, use an ice cube or ice Popsicle to paint on pages from a "paint with water" book. Or place a "paint with water" page in a baking pan, add an ice cube, and let your child move the pan around and watch the picture come to life.

Squeeze Painting

Flour
Salt
Water
Food colouring or liquid tempera paint (optional)
Squeeze bottles (the kind mustard or ketchup comes in) or small spoons
Paper

Mix equal parts of flour, salt, and water. If working on coloured paper, leave the paint white; if using white paper, add a few drops of food colouring or liquid tempera to the paint. Pour the paint into squeeze bottles or use a small spoon to dribble the paint onto the paper. Let dry, and see the sparkly results.

Painted Place Mats

Rubber cement
White construction paper
Tempera paint
Paintbrushes
Clear contact paper

Dribble rubber cement randomly or in a design over a sheet of white construction paper. Allow to dry for about thirty minutes, then paint over the rubber cement using tempera paint in one or more colours. Allow the paint to dry, then peel the rubber cement off the construction paper to see the design that is left.

Cling Wrap Painting

White paper
Paint
Spoons
Plastic cling wrap

Dribble paint onto the paper with a spoon. Use several different colours. Place a sheet of plastic cling wrap over the paint (make sure the cling wrap covers the whole surface). Use your hands to smooth the cling wrap over the paper, then carefully peel it off. Allow painting to dry.

Feather Painting

For this activity you can use colourful feathers from the craft store or bird feathers you find outside.

Feathers
Glue
Tempera paint
Paper

Mix a little bit of glue with the tempera paint. Use feathers to brush the paint onto the paper. If you like, leave a few feathers on the painting to make a feather collage (when the paint dries, the glue mixed with it will make the feathers stick). You can also try this with pine branches, leaves, flowers, or other natural objects that may be good for painting.

Rainbow Painting

The wet paper really makes the colours flow and blend for a beautiful effect.

> Paper
> Water
> Wide paintbrush or sponge
> Paints or washable markers

Paint a sheet of paper with water using a wide paintbrush or a wet sponge. Your child can paint lines of colour across the page with paints, or draw on it with washable markers.

Salad Spinner Art

A good activity for older toddlers. You may want to donate your salad spinner to the craft box after you do this activity.

> Salad spinner
> Paper plate
> Paint

Remove the plastic insert from the salad spinner and place a small paper plate in the bottom. Replace the insert on top of the paper plate. Dribble a little paint into the spinner, put the lid on, and spin. If you like, add another colour or two and spin some more for a nice effect.

Paint Pen

This is an idea from *Surviving Your Preschooler,* but it is such a great idea for toddlers that I thought it worth repeating.

> Empty roll-on deodorant bottle or shoe polish bottle
> Liquid tempera paint

To make a giant paint pen for your child, pry the top off of a roll-on deodorant or shoe polish bottle. Fill with tempera paint (mixed fairly thickly) and snap the top back on the bottle. Your child can use this for a quick and easy painting activity.

For an easy alternative, use bingo dabbers already filled with ink. The downside is the ink isn't washable and doesn't flow as well as paint.

String Painting

Yarn or string
Scissors
Tape
Popsicle sticks
Liquid tempera paint
Paper

Tape 5-inch pieces of yarn or string to the end of a Popsicle stick. Using the stick as a handle, dip the string into liquid tempera paint and drag it across and around the paper.

Frosty Snow Painting

1 cup powdered laundry soap
½ cup cold water
Electric mixer or wire whisk
Food colouring (optional)
Paintbrushes
Heavy paper or cardboard

Beat or whisk cold water and laundry soap together until stiff. Add food colouring, or leave white if using coloured paper. Paint with a brush or use as fingerpaint on heavy paper or cardboard. Let dry flat.

Corn Cob Painting

If fresh corn isn't available, use a dried corn cob for this activity.

> Paper
> Flat box (the kind a 24-pack of pop comes in) or large baking pan
> Liquid tempera paint
> Flat container for paint (big enough to fit the corn)
> Corn cob (husk removed)
> Clear contact paper (optional)

Place a sheet of paper in the flat box or baking pan. Pour the liquid tempera paint into a shallow, flat container. Place one whole cob of corn into the paint. Roll the corn around so that it is completely covered with paint. Place the paint-covered cob in the box with the paper and let your child rotate the box around so that the cob rolls from side to side. If you like, use another cob of corn in a different colour paint and repeat the rolling process until your child decides she's done.

Let the painting dry. If you like, cover with clear contact paper and use as a place mat.

Rock Painting

> Shoebox with lid or diaper-wipe container
> Paper
> Scissors
> Tempera paint
> Rock
> Golf ball or Ping-Pong ball (optional)

Cut a piece of plain or construction paper to fit the bottom of the shoebox or diaper-wipe container. Pour a small amount of paint into a dish and dip a rock in the paint. Place the rock in the shoebox or container and shut the lid. Shake the box up and down and from side to side. Open the lid and look at the design the rock has made. Dip the rock in another colour of paint and repeat the shaking action until your child tires of this activity.

If you like, substitute a golf or Ping-Pong ball for the rock in this activity.

Paint Dancing

Large sheet or piece of fabric
Baking pan or tray for paint
Liquid tempera paint
Warm, soapy water
Towels
Music

Tape a large sheet or piece of fabric securely to the floor or, better yet, lay it on the ground outside. Fill a baking pan or tray with paint. Add a little liquid soap or dish detergent to make cleanup easier. Put on some music and roll up your child's pant legs, or dress her in only a diaper or shorts. Have her step into the tray of paint, then onto the bedsheet. Then have her dance to the music! Have a pan of warm, soapy water and a towel on hand for when she tires of this activity (or if she refuses to stay on the sheet).

Fingerpainting

Fingerpaints
Fingerpaint or butcher paper

Fingerpainting is a wonderfully messy adventure that every child should experience after about the age of two (or younger, if you can stand it!). Unfortunately, it can be frustrating for parents, as the amount of work required to set up and clean up never seems to merit the five minutes (or less) most children will spend at this activity! That said, be prepared for a great big mess, and make sure your child wears an art smock. Wet the paper first to allow the paint to slide better. Drop a blob of paint on the paper and let your child go to it. Commercial fingerpaint can be bought, or you can make your own using the recipes in Appendix A.

For variety, use fingerpaint that has been chilled or warmed. Add salt or sand for texture. Thick fingerpaint or fingerpaint mixed with salt or sand can also be pushed around the paper with a Popsicle stick or spoon.

If you like, have your child fingerpaint on a tabletop or highchair tray, then press a piece of paper over the paint to make a print to save. Plastic cafeteria trays are great surfaces for fingerpainting, or try it on a window or mirror (a little liquid detergent added to the paint makes cleanup easier).

Bathtub Fingerpainting

This is a great idea for the very youngest artists in your house. If you have ceramic tile around your bathtub, substitute pudding for fingerpaint, as the paint may stain your grout.

> Fingerpaint
> Large sheet of paper

Dress your one-year-old in a diaper and an old shirt. Place her in a dry bathtub with a blob of fingerpaint and watch the results! When her work is complete, lay a large piece of paper over it, press gently, and lift for a copy of her masterpiece.

Shaving Cream Fingerpaint

I wouldn't advise this activity for children with sensitive skin or for those prone to licking their fingers! If you like, substitute whipped cream or instant pudding.

> Shaving cream
> Food colouring or tempera paint

Squirt some shaving cream onto a table top, highchair tray, or piece of paper. Add a few drops of food colouring or sprinkle a bit of powdered tempera paint for instant fingerpaint fun.

Food Colouring Fingerpaint

Food colouring will stain your child's fingers for a day or two, so avoid this activity if your child needs to look her best shortly after your fun.

> Corn syrup
> Brush
> Food colouring
> Heavy paper or posterboard

Spread corn syrup over a piece of heavy paper or posterboard. Drop a few drops of food colouring in various colours onto the paper. Your child will have fun spreading the colours around with her fingers. When the picture dries, it will be shiny and beautiful!

PRINTMAKING

Printmaking involves making an impression of an object onto paper or another surface. The object to be printed can be dipped into paint, covered in paint using a brush or paint roller, or pressed on a print pad.

A print pad can be made by padding up newspaper and soaking it in liquid tempera paint. Or you can place a thin sponge in a shallow tray or small bowl and cover with several tablespoons of paint. For some printmaking, a rubber stamp pad can be used. To cushion the print, place a newspaper under the paper on which the impression is to be made.

Many different types of paper can be used for printing: newsprint, construction paper, and brown paper bags are some of the cheaper options. As with many of the painting projects in this chapter, you can use these printing activities to create some great, environmentally friendly giftwrap.

Very young toddlers are not likely to understand the printmaking process. They tend to use the object to be printed more like a sponge or paintbrush, and usually end up just pushing it around the paper. Older two- and three-year-olds will enjoy making prints. Encourage them to press the object gently into the paint and then onto the paper to make a successful print.

Glue Printing

Remind your child to gently press the object to be printed into the glue then onto the paper so that a clear print of the object is made.

> Various objects for printing with
> White glue
> Glitter, coloured sand, jelly powder, or Kool-Aid drink mix crystals
> Paper

Instead of using paint or a stamp pad for printing, use glue and glitter instead. Press objects (fruit and vegetables cut in half, sponges cut into shapes, string wrapped around a block of wood, and so on) into glue, then onto paper. Sprinkle with glitter (or use coloured sand, jelly powder, or Kool-Aid drink mix) and let dry. Large pieces of newsprint covered with glitter make nice wrapping paper.

Bubble Wrap Printing

Bubble wrap packing material
Tape
Liquid tempera paint (several different colours)
Paintbrush
Paper

Tape the bubble wrap to the table or surface you will be painting on. Have your child paint on the bubble wrap, then press a piece of paper down on it to get an interesting print.

Cardboard Printing

Corrugated cardboard
Scissors or utility knife
Tape or elastic bands
Liquid tempera paint
Construction paper

Cut a piece of corrugated cardboard about six inches wide by ten inches long, cutting the width parallel to the ripples or strips in the cardboard. Roll up the cardboard, beginning the roll on the short side of the rectangle (so that you are not rolling against the corrugated strips). Secure the roll with tape or an elastic band. Dip the end of the cardboard roll into the paint and press onto paper to make a flower-like print.

Berry Basket Printing

Pint-sized berry baskets
Liquid tempera paint
Flat containers for paint
Paper

Pour a small amount of paint into flat containers big enough to fit the berry basket. Place the berry basket, bottom side down, into the paint. Make prints on the paper by pressing the paint-covered bottom of the basket to the paper. Change colours if you like.

Muffin Tin Printing

Muffin tin
Liquid tempera paint (several different colours)
Paintbrush
Paper

Place a muffin tin upside down on a covered surface. Have your child paint the bottoms of the muffin cups. When she's done, place a piece of paper over the muffin tin and press to make a print of her work.

Block Printing

Small blocks of wood
Rickrack
Glue
Liquid tempera paint in a shallow pan
Paper

Glue rickrack to the end of a block of wood. Press the block into the paint then onto paper to make a zigzag design. Move the block around in different directions, and add different colours of paint if you like.

For an alternate activity, wrap string around a block or glue objects such as a key or small plastic ring to the end of the block to make an interesting print design.

Cork Printing

Wine bottle corks
Liquid tempera paint in a shallow pan
Paper

Grasp the cork at one end and hold it upright. Press the cork into the paint then onto a piece of paper or newspaper. If you like, use tempera paint in several different colours.

Toy Car Printing

Toy cars or trucks with wide wheels
Liquid tempera paint
Paper

Pour a small amount of paint in a container big enough to dip the wheels of the toy car or truck in. Place the car or truck into the paint and roll it back and forth a time or two so that the wheels are covered with paint. Roll the car or truck across the paper to make tire tracks.

Duplo Printing

Duplo pieces in different sizes
Liquid tempera paint
Paper

Pour a small amount of paint in a container big enough to dip the Duplo in. Place the Duplo upside down in the paint. Press the paint-covered Duplo onto the paper to make a print. Use both sides of the Duplo and different colours of paint for an interesting print design.

Spool Printing

Print pad or liquid tempera paint
Empty thread spools
Paper

Press empty thread spools onto a print pad or dip them in liquid tempera paint. Press onto paper to make the shape of a tire.

Sponge Printing

Sponge
Chalk
Water
Paper

Soak a sponge in water and squeeze to release the excess. Use a piece of chalk to draw on the wet sponge. Press the wet sponge onto a piece of white or coloured construction paper to create a print. If you like, use chalk in various colours and a variety of sponges in different shapes and sizes.

TEARING, GLUING, AND STICKING

Toddlers, paper, and glue are a great combination. What child hasn't discovered early in life the special joy of scrunching and tearing paper? Keep a stack of old magazines on hand for tearing (most toddlers and young preschoolers can't yet handle a pair of scissors, so avoid frustration altogether and tear everything).

Gluing is great fun, too. Toddlers enjoy the glue itself as much as whatever it is you're having them make. Vary the type of glue your child uses: a glue stick, glue in a bottle, or spreadable paste. Pour a small amount of white glue into a baby food jar lid and add a drop or two of food colouring. Use a small paintbrush or cotton swab to spread the glue around. Provide your child with lots of interesting things to stick: greeting cards, fabric scraps, and paper scraps (tissue, wrapping, construction). You can also use pasta, yarn, cotton balls, and bits of ribbon. Outdoor walks can yield a wonderful supply of new materials including leaves, pine needles, flower petals, and so on. You should also vary the surface onto which your child sticks her things: paper plates, cardboard pieces, egg cartons, empty tissue boxes, and paper of all shapes, sizes, and colours.

The most important thing about gluing and pasting is that your child should do the whole project by herself. Varying the materials used will keep the same basic activity interesting for both you and your child.

Fruit Loop Sand

> Fruit Loop cereal
> Food processor or rolling pin
> Construction paper
> Glue stick

Make Fruit Loop Sand by crushing Fruit Loop cereal in a food processor or with a rolling pin. Rub the glue stick onto a piece of construction paper, then sprinkle the Fruit Loop sand on it. If your child dumps the sand onto the picture all at once, that's okay, just tip the picture onto another piece of paper and the excess will slide off. For variety, use a clean, empty spice container to shake the Fruit Loop sand onto the glue.

Fruit Loop sand can be used in place of glitter for many gluing activities.

Giftwrap Collage

> Giftwrap
> Tissue paper
> Scissors
> Construction paper
> Glue stick
> Clear contact paper (optional)

Save pieces of giftwrap and tissue paper from birthdays and other gift-giving occasions. Cut or tear the paper into interesting shapes and save in a box or Ziploc bag.

Show your child how to rub the glue stick onto a piece of paper, and then how to press a colourful paper shape onto the glued area. If you like, use a piece of clear contact paper taped to the table sticky side up in place of the construction paper and glue.

Popcorn Picture

    Popped popcorn
    Glue stick or white glue
    Construction paper
    Small paper bag (optional)
    Tempera paint powder (optional)

Rub the glue stick on a piece of construction paper, or spread white glue with a brush. Stick popped popcorn onto the construction paper to make a collage. For a winter scene, use plain white popcorn. For spring blossoms, shake popcorn in a small paper bag with powdered tempera paint, then glue the popcorn onto a flower shape cut from construction paper. For variety, try using Cheerios or puffed rice cereal instead.

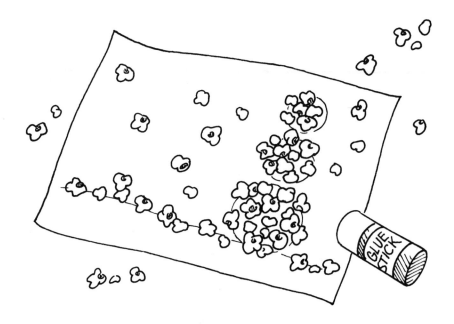

Paper Bag Faces

Some toddlers may lose interest in this activity once the paper bag is stuffed. That's okay, because the real value of this activity for the toddler is in the tearing of paper.

> Newspaper or old magazines for tearing
> Paper bag
> Rubber band
> Crayon, marker, or paint

Tear up old newspapers or magazines. Crumple up the pieces and stuff them in a paper bag. When the bag is full, close the end with a rubber band. Draw or paint a big, happy face on the paper bag. The stuffed paper bag, large and lightweight, is an ideal object for your toddler to lift, carry, or throw.

Tissue Paper Collage

> Tin foil
> Coloured tissue paper
> Scissors (optional)
> Baby oil
> Paintbrush

Tear off a piece of tin foil about the size of a piece of paper. Cut or tear the tissue paper into small pieces. Squeeze a few drops of baby oil onto the tin foil and spread around with a paintbrush. Show your child how the tissue paper will stick to the foil wherever the baby oil is, but can be easily removed. Use different colours of tissue paper to make a collage.

Salt Pictures

> Salt (or clean sand)
> Tempera paint powder
> Empty salt and pepper shakers or spice containers
> Paper
> Glue
> Paintbrush or spoon

Mix salt or sand with tempera paint powder in small shaker-type containers, one for each colour. Brush glue onto paper with a small brush or dribble it on with a spoon. (Little ones may enjoy smearing the glue around with their fingers.) Sprinkle the salt/paint mixture over the paper. When glue is dry, tip off the excess salt and hang to display.

Coloured salt or sand can be used in place of glitter for many gluing activities.

Glitter Shapes

Construction paper
Scissors
Glue stick
Glitter or confetti
Small shoebox with lid
Rubber bands

Cut shapes out of construcion paper. Make basic geometric shapes such as circles, squares, triangles, or rectangles, or seasonal shapes such as hearts, pumpkins, candy canes, and so on. Rub the glue stick on one or both sides of a shape. Put the glue-covered shape into the shoebox along with confetti or glitter. Place the lid on the shoebox and secure with a couple of rubber bands. Shake the box to cover the shape with glitter or confetti. Remove the shape from the box and allow to dry.

Tape Collage

Tape (masking, cellophane, coloured, and so on)
Small can or plastic container
Construction paper

Use an upside-down can (such as a tuna can) or plastic container as a tape holder for your child. Cut or tear off various lengths of tape and place them around the edges of the tape holder so that your child can pull them off easily. Use as many different types and colours of tape as you can. Give your child a piece of construction paper and show her how to pull a piece of tape off the tape holder and stick it onto the paper to make a collage.

Waxed Paper Art

A safer and easier alternative to using grated crayons and an iron.

> Glue
> Liquid tempera paint or food colouring
> Paintbrush
> Waxed paper
> Colourful leaves

Mix glue with tempera paint or food colouring to achieve a bright colour (or use coloured glue thinned with a little water). Use a brush to paint glue onto two pieces of waxed paper of the same size (the paper should be well covered with glue). Stick colourful leaves onto the glue on one piece of paper, then cover with the other sheet. Press together to stick, then hang in a window.

Pathfinding

This is an excellent activity for developing small muscles. Using scissors is too tough for young toddlers, but older two- or three-year-olds can definitely give it a try. If paper is too difficult to cut, try playdough instead.

> Pen or pencil
> Paper
> Child's scissors

Draw an easy-to-cut pattern (using two lines to form a path) on a plain piece of paper. Paths could follow a variety of shapes: zigzag, S-shape, straight lines, and so on. Have your child cut right down the centre of the path without straying. If you like, keep your child's cutting exercises in a special folder that you can add to each day.

Spaghetti Mobiles

If your child is likely to eat the glue-covered noodles, substitute corn syrup thinned with a little water for the glue. Many toddlers will enjoy just playing with warm spaghetti noodles on a highchair tray or tabletop.

White glue (or corn syrup)
Food colouring in two or three different colours
Containers for glue
Cooked spaghetti noodles
Styrofoam meat tray
Yarn or ribbon

Decide how many colours of glue you want to make, and pour glue into that many containers. Add a few drops of food colouring to each glue container, using a different colour for each container. Show your child how to dip the spaghetti, one piece at a time, into the coloured glue, and lay it on the styrofoam meat tray. Repeat, using different colours of glue, until your child tires of this activity. Let the noodles dry, then remove from the meat tray, tie on a piece of yarn or ribbon, and hang from the ceiling as a mobile.

CRAFTS AND OTHER FUN THINGS TO MAKE

Craft projects will challenge your child's imagination and artistic ability, and they will facilitate the development of small muscle skills. They may also fill in the long hours of a rainy day, keeping your child stimulated and happy.

Don't forget that, with toddlers, it's the process that counts—not the product. Don't be discouraged if your child won't do it the "right" way. Perhaps she's still too young to be working on these crafts, or perhaps you need to let her freely explore the craft materials she's using and create a masterpiece of her own.

Toddler Collage

You may do this activity in one sitting, or spread it out over a couple of days by adding interesting objects as you find them.

> Clear contact paper
> Scissors
> Variety of objects to stick
> Construction paper (optional)
> Cardboard box (optional)
> Tape (optional

Cut two pieces of clear contact paper about the size of a piece of paper, or larger if you like. Remove the backing from one piece of contact paper and lay it on a flat surface such as a table or highchair tray, sticky side up. Tape the corners to the table or highchair tray so that the contact paper won't move around. (If you're planning on working on the collage over a couple of days, tape the contact paper to a cardboard box that can be moved out of the way when you're not working on it.)

Provide a variety of interesting objects for your toddler to stick to the contact paper. Use scraps of tissue or wrapping paper, bits of colourful yarn or ribbon, small pieces of pasta, cotton balls, or leaves or flower petals. When her collage is done, cover it with the other piece of contact paper, or use a piece of construction paper instead. Hang in a window or on the wall for all to admire, or use as a unique place mat.

Artwork Display

Here's a way to display your child's artwork on the refrigerator without having to cover it up with magnets to keep it there!

> Wooden ruler (12-, 18-, or 24-inch)
> Magnetic strip (same length as the ruler)
> Glue gun
> Clothespins, spring-type (at least two)

Glue the magnetic strip to the back of the wooden ruler. Glue spring-type clothespins to the front of the ruler so that the pins open downward. Use two clothespins for a 12-inch ruler, placing one at each end. You may want to use three or four clothespins for a longer ruler. Write your child's name with marker or glitter on the front of the ruler, or let your child decorate the ruler and clothespins with paint, glitter, pasta, and so on. When dry, place the ruler on the refrigerator and clip your child's artwork with the clothespins.

Sticker Art

Stickers come in handy for making quick crafts and matching games, decorating cards and gifts, making charts, and so on. Children of all ages love stickers. Now is the time to begin a collection, if you haven't started one already.

> Stickers
> Paper
> Paper plate (optional)
> Small pop bottle or plastic vitamin bottle (optional)

Show your child how to peel the sticker off the backing and press it to a piece of paper. To make a wallhanging, press stickers to a paper plate. Make a vase by decorating a small pop or plastic vitamin bottle with stickers. You can colour on plain white labels to make your own stickers.

Fishy Beanbag

Your child will have as much fun helping you make this easy beanbag as she will playing with it after.

> Tube sock
> Dried beans
> Yarn
> Marker
> Glue
> Felt scraps (optional)

Fill a child-sized tube sock about three-quarters full with dried beans. Tie tightly with yarn to make a tail. Push in the toe of the sock to form the mouth, and insert glue to hold the shape. Use a marker to draw on eyes and gills, or you can cut eyes, gills, and fins from scraps of felt and glue them to the sock. Use the fishy beanbag to play catch, or try to throw it in an empty laundry basket.

Book Mark

Another great gift idea for grandparents, or use as unique thank-you cards for gifts your child has received.

> Pencil for tracing
> Paper
> Scissors
> Crayons, markers, stickers, and glitter for decorating
> Clear contact paper

Place your child's hand and arm on a piece of paper and trace around it. Cut the tracing out of paper and have your child decorate it with crayons, markers, stickers, glitter, and so on. Be sure to write your child's name and age or date on the back. Cover with clear contact paper and use for a book mark.

Footprint T-Shirt

This makes a great gift for moms, dads, and grandparents.

> Fabric paint
> Paintbrush
> White T-shirt

Paint your child's feet and press them onto a white T-shirt. You can paint them different colours and press them randomly over the shirt, or use one colour and make a trail of footprints up the front and down the back of the shirt. Personalize the T-shirt even more with a scanned, iron-on photograph or a special message written in fabric paint.

Fishy Necklace

This makes a great seasonal activity, too. Instead of fish, cut holidays shapes such as hearts or shamrocks.

> Uncooked tube-shaped pasta, dyed or painted in bright colours
> Construction paper
> Hole punch
> Shoelace (18-inch or longer)
> Scissors

Cut 3- to 4-inch long fish shapes from various colours of construction paper; punch a hole for an eye in each fish. Show your child how to string the painted or dyed pasta alternately with the fish shapes onto the shoelace; tie ends together to make a necklace. (Instead of using tube-shaped pasta, you can use straws cut into 1-inch lengths, but these will be more difficult for toddlers to string.)

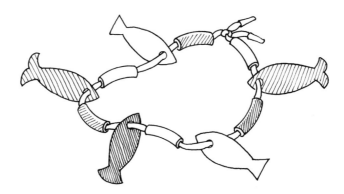

Bedtime Buddy

Roll of drawing paper
Pen or marker
Old sheet
Scissors
Sewing machine or needle and thread
Cotton batting
Fabric paint

Have your child lie down on a large piece of drawing paper and trace around her body. Cut out the outline and use it as a pattern to cut two body outlines out of an old sheet. Sew them together, right sides in, leaving enough space to turn the right sides out. Turn, stuff with cotton batting, and sew the hole closed. Decorate with fabric paint and dress in your child's clothes.

CHAPTER ELEVEN

Birthday and Holiday Activities

Of course, parents don't have children because they want to be martyrs, or at least they shouldn't. They have them because they love children and want some of their very own. They also love children because they remember being loved so much by their parents in their childhood. Taking care of their children, seeing them grow and develop into fine people, gives most parents—despite the hard work—their greatest satisfaction in life. DR. BENJAMIN SPOCK

Holiday celebrations provide an important break from the day-to-day routine for children and adults. Whether preparing for a major celebration, such as Christmas or Hanukkah, or simply making green Jell-O for St. Patrick's Day, the anticipation of a special day lifts our spirits and impart a sense of family tradition to our children.

While toddlers are too young to understand much of the significance of each holiday, you can still make the most of each occasion. Begin by talking to your child about the upcoming event. Read simple library books that explain the story of your tradition. Look at video tapes or photo albums of past family celebrations. When the holiday actually arrives, refer to the books you have read or photos you have looked at to help your child make the connection between the story and the event.

Keep in mind that, especially for toddlers, celebrations do not need to be lavish. Bake a special batch of cookies, paint pictures in seasonal colours, or invite friends over for a simple lunch or teddy-bear tea. To get the most out of the holiday, try to be as routine as possible about your child's meals and naps.

This chapter will suggest many ideas for celebrating holidays with toddlers. Many of the activities break my own rule about simplicity—they're a little complex for most toddlers to do on their own. You'll need to assist and, at times, do part of the process yourself. This does limit the learning value for the child, so try to make these activities the exception rather than the rule. But sometimes it's okay to make or do something just because you want to, rather than always wondering and worrying about what your child will learn from it. Toddlers will benefit when you let them do the things they're capable of doing, even if it means they don't do everything by themselves.

BIRTHDAY CELEBRATIONS

Although parents usually do, most toddlers will not get into birthdays in a really big way. For the first few years of life, a family dinner complete with birthday cake and candles is usually sufficient for a birthday celebration. However, if you want to invite a few friends over for a party, keep the festivities simple:

- ▲ Put some playdough or a simple craft out to occupy the children until all the guests have arrived.
- ◀ If there are no other adults on hand, ask the children's parents (or at least one or two) to stay for the party. They'll be a very big help to you when it's time to organize the children for food, games, or circle time.
- ▶ Serve a simple meal of sandwiches or hotdogs, vegetable sticks, and juice or chocolate milk. If you plan the party for midmorning or afternoon, put out a fruit platter and juice or milk with the birthday cake.
- ◀ Most toddlers are too young to enjoy group games, but sitting in a circle and singing songs or doing a few simple finger plays can be great fun.
- ▼ After an hour and a half or two hours of eating, singing, playing, and opening gifts, most little guests will be ready to depart. Have your child say good-bye to each guest individually as they leave.

Although sending thank-you notes may be an old-fashioned custom, it's one I started with my children long before they could understand the concept, and it's one I hope they will continue into adulthood (good manners and gratitude are never out of date). Use a piece of your child's artwork as an original thank-you card. Write the message yourself and, if you like, enclose a photograph of your child with each card.

Birthday Memory Book

Construction paper
Stapler
Crayons or markers
Stickers and glitter for decorating
Birthday photographs
Clear contact paper (optional)
Birthday cards and memorabilia
Glue

Staple or sew together ten (or more) sheets of construction paper to make a birthday memory book for your child. Decorate the front with your child's name, age, date of the birthday, and so on. Add stickers, glitter, and a photograph of the birthday child, and cover with clear contact paper if you like. Inside the book, your child can glue his birthday cards and other reminders of his special day.

Party Tablecloth

You can use this idea to make custom tablecloths for birthdays, holidays, and other special events. Older children may enjoy making a tablecloth with their friends at their next birthday party.

Large roll or sheets of plain newsprint
Paint, crayons, or markers
Clear vinyl tablecloth

Cut a length of paper the size of the table to be covered. Let your children draw on the paper with crayons, markers, or paints. You may want to add stickers, or you can glue pictures cut from magazines. When the masterpiece is complete, place it on the table and cover with a clear vinyl tablecloth.

Video Time Capsule

This idea comes from *Surviving Your Preschooler,* but I have included it here as well. If you like this idea, you'll want to start it as early as possible—your child's first birthday would be the perfect time.

Video camera
Videotape

If you have access to a video camera, consider making a videotape of your child on each birthday throughout his childhood. Beginning on his first birthday (if you can), spend a couple of minutes taping him sitting, crawling, standing, walking, or doing whatever stage he happens to be in. If you like, show his room, his favourite toys and books, and so on. As the years progress and your child becomes more vocal, ask him questions about his favourite foods, songs, activities, friends, and so on. Ask your child what he is looking forward to over the year, and what he expects life to be like next year on his birthday.

When the segment is complete, put the tape away and don't tape on it until next year's birthday. If doing this for more than one child, use a different tape for each, but use the tape only for the time capsule. Years down the road you'll be able to watch your child grow up on his time capsule birthday tape.

VALENTINE'S DAY (February 14th)

Valentine's Day is for celebrating love. Although no one is quite sure how Valentine's Day and its accompanying traditions started, most of us enjoy sharing cards, chocolates, hugs, and kisses with those we love.

Valentine celebrations for toddlers can be kept fairly simple. Read a book about Valentine's Day several times in the days and weeks prior to February 14th. Make simple red, white, and pink decorations to put up around the house. Bake and ice some heart-shaped cookies to give to a friend or neighbour. On Valentine's Day, dress the whole family in red and put your heart-shaped cookie cutter to work for toast, sandwiches, apples, cheese, and finger Jell-O. A small party with a few friends can be a simple and fun way to celebrate this special day.

Jell-O Painting

> One package red Jell-O
> Water
> Construction paper
> Paintbrush
> Scissors

Mix Jell-O with a small amount of water to make a fairly thick, spreadable paste. Cut a heart shape from a piece of construction paper and have your child paint the heart with Jell-O. Let dry. This makes a delicious-smelling valentine card or picture for someone special.

Valentine Cookies

> Rolled cookie dough
> Heart-shaped cookie cutters
> Pink icing
> Sprinkles or other candy to decorate with

Prepare a batch of rolled cookie dough ahead of time. Let your toddler help with some of the simpler aspects of the recipe. Roll the dough out and use a heart-shaped cookie cutter to cut heart shapes from the dough. Bake as directed and let cool. Ice with pink icing and decorate with sprinkles or other candy.

Valentine Postcard

Heavy white paper or postcard
Paper doily
Red or pink paint
Paintbrush or sponge
Clear contact paper (optional)

Place a paper doily on one side of a blank postcard, or on a piece of heavy white paper folded to make a card. You can hold the doily in place with small amount of tacky adhesive or a paper clip. Paint or sponge over the doily and onto the postcard beneath it. Remove the doily and let the postcard dry. Cover with clear contact paper to give it a finished look.

Edible Valentines

Graham wafers
Candy conversation hearts, cinnamon hearts, or other heart-shaped candy
Frosting

Use frosting to glue candy hearts to graham wafers for a completely edible valentine.

Valentine Cupcakes

Use this idea to make heart-shaped cupcakes for Valentine's Day.

> Marbles (one for each cupcake)
> Paper baking cups
> Cake batter
> Frosting
> Sprinkles and other candy for decorating

Wash and dry enough marbles so that there is one for each cupcake you're making. Line a muffin tin with paper baking cups. Place one marble in each section between the side of the paper cup and the tin (the marbles mould the baking cups into heart shapes). Pour in the batter and bake according to the recipe. Cool and decorate with frosting, sprinkles, and other candies.

Sweetheart Sandwiches

> Bread slices
> Softened cream cheese
> Red food colouring
> Heart-shaped cookie cutters
> Honey and/or cinnamon (optional)

Mix softened cream cheese with a drop or two of red food colouring. Add more food colouring, one drop at a time, if you want a darker colour. If you like, flavor the cream cheese with honey and/or cinnamon. Spread the coloured cream cheese on slices of bread. Use cookie cutters to cut out heart-shaped sandwiches.

Valentine Hearts

> Pink construction paper
> Scissors
> Red and white liquid tempera paint
> Spoons
> Small rolling pin (optional)

Cut out large heart shapes from construction paper; fold in half then open up again. Have your child use a spoon to dribble red and white liquid tempera paint onto the heart. Fold the heart up with the paint on the inside; your child can use his hand or a small rolling pin to press on the top of the folded heart. Open up the heart again to see the designs the paint has made. You can write on the unpainted side of the heart, or glue it onto another sheet of white or red construction paper to make pretty Valentine's Day cards.

ST. PATRICK'S DAY (March 17th)

St. Patrick's Day is set aside to honour the patron saint of Ireland. Bishop Patrick introduced Christianity to Ireland during the fifth century, and in Ireland he is still honoured with a national holiday and a week of religious festivities.

Whether you're Irish or not, St. Patrick's Day can help break up the monotony of the last days of winter. Dress in green and invite a few friends over for a small St. Patrick's Day celebration. Make a craft together and play a few simple games. Serve green food such as cupcakes or sugar cookies with green icing (or decorate them as a party activity). Colour white grape juice green with a drop or two of food colouring, or serve limeade or green Kool-Aid. Wind up the day with your own St. Patrick's Day parade, either in your livingroom or outside if the weather is fine.

Potato Press Picture

Very young children tend to use the potato like a paintbrush or sponge, pushing it around the paper. Remind your child to press the potato gently into the paint than onto the paper to make a successful print.

    Raw potato, cut in half
    Shallow dish of green tempera paint
    Construction paper

Dip the cut surface of the potato into the green paint and press onto the construction paper. Repeat until the paper is covered with green shapes. Use as a St. Patrick's Day card or picture.

Shamrock Necklace

Green and white construction paper
Scissors
Hole punch
Shoelaces, ribbon, or yarn for stringing

Cut several sizes of shamrocks from green and white construction paper. Punch a hole in the top of each shamrock. Give your child a shoelace (or length of ribbon, or yarn with masking tape wrapped on one end) and show him how to string the shamrocks to make a St. Patrick's Day necklace.

Shamrock Rubbings

Sandpaper
Scissors
Crayons (paper removed)
Paper

Cut shamrock shapes out of sandpaper. Use different grains of sandpaper and cut the shamrocks in several different sizes. Tape the shamrocks to a table. Show your child how to place his paper over the shamrock and rub with the side of a crayon to get a St. Patrick's Day design.

EASTER (Date Varies)

Easter is a joyous celebration, the traditional Christian holiday that celebrates the resurrection of Jesus Christ. It is also a time to celebrate the coming of spring and all the delightful signs of new life that abound. Easter is a great time for family dinners and small get-togethers with friends. Decorate Easter eggs together or make a simple Easter craft. Hold an Easter egg or candy hunt outdoors or in, depending on the weather. Have an informal parade in your neighbourhood with decorated wagons and tricycles. This is another wonderful holiday that helps break the monotony of the last few days of winter, so start your Easter crafts and activities early.

Easy Easter Eggs

These Easter eggs are easy enough for even the littlest hands to make.

> Cotton swabs
> Cotton balls
> Liquid tempera paint
> Hard-boiled eggs
> Clear acrylic spray (optional)

Dip a cotton swab or cotton ball in paint and use to dab paint on the hard-boiled egg. For a shiny finish, spray with clear acrylic spray.

Easter Egg Holder

This is an easy way to display all the eggs your child decorates.

> Empty paper towel roll
> Scissors
> Construction paper
> Glue
> Glitter or stickers for decorating

Cut the paper towel roll into 2-inch sections. Cut strips of construction paper two inches wide and long enough to wrap around the paper towel roll. Glue the construction paper strips to the pieces of paper towel roll, and decorate with glitter or stickers.

Tissue Paper Eggs

Coloured tissue paper
White craft glue
Hard-boiled eggs
Clear acrylic spray (optional)

Tear coloured tissue paper into small pieces. Dilute white craft glue with a few drops of water. Have your child spread glue on the hard-boiled egg with his fingers. After he has washed his hands, show him how to gently press pieces of tissue paper onto the egg. Cover with a light coating of glue or spray with clear acrylic spray.

Easter Bouquet

Paper baking cups
Scissors
Pipe cleaners
Glue
Ribbon
Glitter

Poke a hole with scissors or a pen through the bottom of the baking cup. Stick a pipe cleaner through the hole. Bend the top of the pipe cleaner over and glue into place. Spread glue over the paper baking cup and decorate with glitter. Bunch together four or five flowers, twisting the pipe cleaner stems together. Tie with ribbon to make a springtime bouquet.

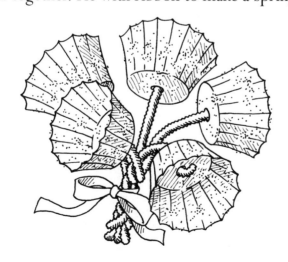

Tissue Easter Egg

Coloured tissue paper cut into 3-inch squares
Construction paper
Scissors
Glue

Cut an egg shape from a piece of construction paper. Show your child how to wad the tissue paper square, dip it in glue, and stick it to the egg.

Easter Egg Pick-Up

Tissue paper
Pie plate
Plastic drinking straws
Scissors

Cut several tissue paper eggs about three inches long. Place the eggs in a pie plate. Show your child how to put the straw in his mouth and take a deep breath, seeing how many eggs he can pick up on the end of the straw.

Easter Egg Necklace

Construction paper in several different colours
Scissors
Hole punch
Shoelace, ribbon, or yarn
Crayons, markers, stickers (optional)
Glue, glitter, sequins (optional)

Cut out some egg-shaped pieces of construction paper in several different colours. Punch a hole in the top of each egg. If you like, decorate with crayons, markers, stickers, glitter, or sequins. Show your child how to slip the end of the shoelace through the holes in the eggs to make a necklace. You'll need to tie something temporarily onto one end of the shoelace to make sure the eggs don't fall off the other end as he adds them. If using ribbon or yarn, taping the end makes it easier for little fingers to thread it through the hole.

CANADA DAY (July 1st)

Canada Day on July 1st celebrates the anniversary of our country's confederation in 1867, and so this holiday is Canada's birthday. Canada Day celebrations differ from family to family, although traditions usually include a parade, picnic or barbecue with family and friends, and fireworks at night.

Most toddlers won't understand the significance of their own birthday, so celebrating the birthday of a country is not a concept they will easily grasp. You can, however, do simple things to begin building Canada Day traditions with your child. Make a birthday card for Canada using some of your child's artwork. Bake a birthday cake, light a few candles, and sing, "Happy Birthday, Canada." Fly the flag proudly. Decorate your house and dress your children with a red and white theme. Your family's Canada Day traditions and celebrations will help your children feel proud of their country.

Fireworks Printing

Two plastic scouring pads (one for each colour)
Red and white liquid tempera paint
Two flat containers (one for each colour)
Black construction paper

Pour the paint into two flat containers. Dip a plastic scouring pad into one of the paint containers and press it onto a piece of black construction paper. (Encourage your child to press gently rather than pound his scouring pad onto the paper.) Continue dipping and pressing, using red and white to create a Canada Day fireworks picture.

Maple Leaf Sponge Painting

Maple-leaf-shaped sponge
Red liquid tempera paint
White construction paper

Dip the maple-leaf-shaped sponge into red liquid tempera paint. Press onto a piece of white construction paper for a "Maple Leaf" painting.

Canada Day Salad

Bananas
Raspberries or strawberries
Vanilla yogourt

Slice bananas. Combine with raspberries or strawberries and vanilla yogourt in a small bowl. Mix and serve.

Flag Snacks

Graham wafers
White frosting
Two small containers
Red food colouring
Small plastic knives or Popsicle sticks

Divide white frosting equally into two small containers. Add a few drops of red food colouring to one container. Mix well. If you like, add more food colouring until the desired shade is reached. Show your toddler how to use a small plastic knife or Popsicle stick to spread the coloured frosting onto graham wafers.

THANKSGIVING (Second Monday in October)

The first Thanksgiving celebration was held by the Pilgrims after their first harvest in 1621. Although many of the original settlers died that first year, the remaining Pilgrims were grateful for the abundance of their harvest and invited the natives around them to join in their three-day feast.

Thanksgiving celebrations today usually include a huge family meal of roast turkey and all the trimmings. Although your toddler will not understand the significance of this holiday, it is never too early to begin to cultivate a spirit of thankfulness in your child. He may not understand all that you say, but you can still talk with your child about all that you have for which you are thankful.

You can also begin to encourage a giving spirit in your child. Donate canned food to the food bank. It's a simple act that will positively impact your community. Prepare for Thanksgiving each year by setting aside good, usable cothing and toys, then take them to a local relief agency. Bake a plate of cookies for housebound friends or community workers. Several years ago we surprised the garbage collectors one morning with a plate of brownies. My kids still talk about it!

Dry Leaf Collage

Construction paper
Scissors
Dry leaves
Glue stick

Cut one or two leaf shapes out of construction paper. Crinkle up dry leaves until they're in fairly small pieces (this may be your toddler's favourite part). Spread glue on one side of the construction paper leaf and sprinkle with dry leaf pieces. If you like, punch a hole in the construction paper and hang to display.

Rainbow Turkey

Brown, red, yellow, and green paint
Paper
Markers

Paint your child's palm and thumb brown, then paint across his fingers (like a rainbow) strips of red, yellow, and green. Press his hand on a piece of paper to make a turkey print. When the paint is dry, use markers to add the eye, beak, and wattle.

Thanksgiving Place Mat

Old magazines
Construction paper or light cardboard
Glue or paste
Clear contact paper

Give your child old magazines and have him cut out pictures of things for which he is thankful. Let him glue them onto a piece of cardboard or construction paper and cover with clear contact paper for a Thanksgiving place mat.

Thanksgiving Turkey

Construction paper or small paper plate
Marker or pencil
Glue
Dried beans and uncooked pasta

Trace around your child's hand (fingers spread out) on a piece of construction paper or small paper plate. Using the pen or marker, draw an eye, beak, and wattle on the thumb, and turkey feet at the bottom of the traced hand. Decorate by gluing on dried beans and uncooked pasta.

Feather Printing

Sponges
Scissors
Liquid tempera paint (in fall colours)
Water
Paper

Cut feather shapes in various sizes out of sponges, being sure to include the stem on the end of the feather shape you cut. Wet sponges, squeeze out, dip into paint, and press onto large sheets of paper. The different sizes and colours of feathers create a nice effect.

HALLOWEEN (October 31st)

Halloween began in ancient times as a pagan celebration of the arrival of winter. It was then that the Lord of Death called together all the souls of the wicked who had died during the past year. The Druids believed that on this night ghosts, goblins, and witches would appear and harm people. Huge bonfires and masks were meant to frighten away these evil beings. People dressed in costumes of animals skins so that the spirits wouldn't recognize them. Special food left on the doorstep to appease the spirits began our tradition of trick-or-treating.

Despite its frightening origins, Halloween has become a fun tradition for many people—adults and children alike. As with most other holidays, toddlers are too young to understand the significance of Halloween. They can, however, be easily frightened by some of the activities which surround this day, so it's wise to be careful where you take them at this time of year. Local churches and community centres often have a Fall Carnival or party where children can play games, eat food, and have fun without the dangers associated with being on the street. If you want to have a small Halloween party yourself, encourage friends to dress in fun, nonscary costumes. Make a simple craft, then decorate and eat some Halloween cookies, cupcakes, or other treats.

Regardless of how you celebrate this occasion, here are some fun activities for you and your child to do together.

Pumpkin Prints

Very young children tend to use the pumpkin like a sponge or paintbrush, pushing it around the paper. Encourage them to press the pumpkin gently into the paint then onto the paper to make a successful print.

> Very small pumpkin
> Knife
> Orange and black tempera paint
> Paper

Cut a small pumpkin in half and dip it into orange and black paint. Press it onto paper to make a pumpkin print. When the paint dries, cover with clear contact paper for a Halloween place mat, or fold the paper in half to make a Halloween card.

Paper Bag Pumpkin

Paper lunch bag
Newspaper or other paper for crumpling
Twist tie, rubber band, or string
Orange and green tempera paint
Paintbrush
Black marker

Crumple up newspaper or other scraps of paper and stuff the lunch bag until it is about two-thirds full. Close the bag with a twist tie, rubber band, or piece of string. Twist the unstuffed part of the bag to make a stem. Paint the pumpkin part of the bag orange, and paint the stem green. When the paint is dry, draw a face on the pumpkin with a black marker.

Painted Spider's Web

White tempera paint
Black construction paper
Drinking straw

Drop a bit of thin white tempera paint onto the centre of a piece of black construction paper. Give your child a straw and show him how to blow the paint around to make a spider's web.

Jack-O-Orange

Orange
Whole cloves
Black marker

Use a black marker to draw a simple face on an orange. Show your child how to poke the cloves into the orange to make a Halloween face.

Paper Plate Spider's Web

Even if you're not into spiders at Halloween, this is a neat idea for any time of the year.

Paper plate
Pie plate or round cake pan
Black paint
Marble

Place a paper plate inside a metal or aluminum pie plate or round cake pan. Put a small amount of black paint in the centre of the paper plate and drop a marble in. Your child will have fun moving and tilting the pie plate or cake pan from side to side to make a "spider's web" on his plate.

For a variation, paint the paper plate dark blue or black first and use white paint for a more realistic looking spider's web, or use more than one colour of paint for a rainbow spider's web.

CHRISTMAS (December 25th)

Christmas is a time when Christians the world over celebrate the birth of Jesus Christ. For some, Christmas means the arrival of Santa Claus, Father Christmas, Père Noël, or Saint Nicholas. Christmas celebrations usually emphasize family togetherness, doing thoughtful and loving things for others, and lots of good food.

However Christmas is celebrated, most will agree that this time of year often brings with it more than just peace, joy, love, and goodwill. For adults, Christmas often means a time of frenzied activity, extra stress, and financial demands that can be hard to meet. Sometimes unrealistic expectations—those we have of ourselves, those we have of others, and those others have of us—make it hard to truly enjoy the wonders of the season.

At this busy time of year, concentrate on what is important. Spend your time, money, and energy on activities that will build or uphold family traditions and make memories for your child. Don't forget simple pleasures like reading together, singing carols by the Christmas tree, or making a holiday craft. Bake some Christmas cookies together, go for a walk in the snow, and sip hot chocolate by the fire. Children need your time and attention more than anything else. Although your child may soon forget toys and other "things," time spent together makes memories he will treasure for a lifetime.

As with other holiday crafts in this chapter, some of these activities may be too complex for some toddlers. Remember to allow your child to do the parts he is capable of doing. In addition to the ideas which follow, simple painting projects or tissue paper collages in seasonal colours are great Christmas activities for toddlers.

Pencil Holder

Tape and toddlers are a great combination. Your child will have fun making this pencil holder (or vase) as a Christmas gift for a family member or friend.

> Small, clean can
> Masking tape
> Brown liquid shoe polish or tempera paint
> Clear acrylic spray or shellac

Show your toddler how to tear small pieces of masking tape and stick them onto a small can. If your toddler has trouble tearing the tape, tear the tape for him and place the pieces around the rim of an upside-down tuna can or plastic container. When the can is covered with pieces of masking tape, paint with brown liquid shoe polish or tempera paint to create a leathery look. If brown isn't high on your child's list of favourite colours, choose another colour. When the paint or shoe polish is dry, spray with clear acrylic spray, or brush with shellac to give the pencil holder a shiny finish.

Cottonball Snowman

    Cottonballs
    Clear contact paper
    Construction paper
    Scissors
    Stapler

Cut three circles from clear contact paper; the circles should be in three different sizes ranging from a diameter of 1-to-2-inches to 4-to-5-inches. Staple the contact paper, backing side up, to the construction paper to form a snowman shape. Your child can peel off the backing and stick cottonballs to the contact paper to cover the snowman. If you like, cut additional snowman features such as a hat or carrot from construction paper and glue to the snowman.

Christmas Noisemaker

    Empty frozen juice container with metal lid
    Glue gun or tape
    Popped popcorn
    Uncooked white beans

Put uncooked beans and popped popcorn into a clean, dry frozen juice container. Place the metal lid on top and glue or tape securely. If you like, cover the juice container with red or green construction paper and decorate with markers or stickers. Now your child has a Christmas noisemaker to shake, shake, shake.

Rudolph Sandwiches

Sliced bread
Peanut butter
Pretzels
Raisins
Maraschino cherry

Cut a slice of bread into a triangle shape. Spread the triangle of bread with peanut butter (or use jam, honey, or cream cheese according to your child's preference). Add pretzels for antlers, raisins for eyes, and a bright red maraschino cherry for Rudolph's nose.

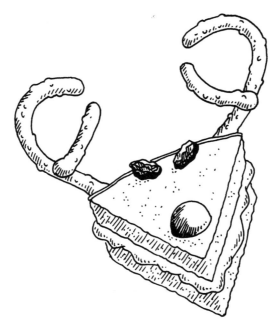

Animal Dress-Up

Stuffed animals or dolls
Christmas ribbon, bows, or fabric

When decorating your home for the holidays, encourage your child to do some decorating of his own. Dress up your child's favourite dolls or stuffed animals with some Christmas ribbon or big, bright bows, or use Christmas fabric to create kerchiefs or scarves. Display the animals on a shelf in your child's room or on a mantel in a more prominent part of your house.

Christmas Tree

Lids from frozen juice cans or baby food jars (at least ten)
Magnet strips
Glue gun
Green felt
Felt in other bright colours
Scissors

Cut small circles of coloured felt to fit the lids. Use lots of green and other colours such as red, yellow, and blue. If using baby food jar lids, glue a circle of felt to the inside of each lid. If using juice container lids, glue the felt to the outside of the lid. Glue a small magnetic strip to the other side of each lid. You can arrange these magnets in the shape of a Christmas tree on your refrigerator door. Your toddler will have fun making designs of his own.

Cinnamon Drawing

Sandpaper
Scissors
Cinnamon sticks

Cut the sandpaper into a holiday shape such as a star, Christmas tree, or gingerbread man. Show your child how to rub the cinnamon stick on the sandpaper to make both a nice design and a pleasing fragrance. If you like, punch a hole at the top of the sandpaper and string yarn through it to make a Christmas tree decoration.

Christmas Doorknob Decoration

Red and green felt
Plastic lid for tracing, about 4-inch diameter
Glue
Stickers, glitter, beads, sequins, and so on

Cut a 4-inch diameter circle out of red felt. Cut out a 1-inch diameter circle in the middle of the red circle, and cut four ½-inch slits around the inner circle to allow it to fit over a doorknob. Cut a 7-inch Christmas tree shape from the green felt. Glue the top of the tree to the bottom of the red felt circle. Your child can decorate his tree with beads, glitter, sequins, stickers, or any other scraps you have on hand.

Stone Paperweight

This paperweight is easy for toddlers to make and a great Christmas gift for someone special.

> Large, smooth stone
> Tempera paint
> Paintbrush
> Clear acrylic spray or shellac
> Glitter (optional)

Go on a walk with your toddler and look for a large, smooth stone. At home, have your child paint the stone in his favourite colours. When dry, finish with clear acrylic spray or shellac for a shiny finish. If you like, sprinkle glitter on the finish before it dries.

Christmas Shapes

> White construction paper
> Scissors
> Red and green tissue paper or giftwrap
> Glue
> Glitter (optional)
> Hole punch (optional)
> Ribbon or yarn (optional)

Cut circles, squares, rectangles, and triangles out of white construction paper. Cut or tear red and green tissue paper or giftwrap into fairly small (about 1-inch) pieces. Spread glue on the construction paper shapes, and press the tissue paper or giftwrap pieces onto the glue. If you like, sprinkle glitter on for a sparkly effect. Punch a hole in the top of each shape, thread a loop of ribbon or yarn through the hole, and hang from doorknobs, or use the shapes to make holiday cards.

Krispie Christmas Treats

    5 cups Rice Krispies
    ¼ cup butter or margarine
    4 cups mini-marshmallows (or 40 large)
    Red or green food colouring
    Metal cookie cutters in Christmas shapes

Melt margarine in a 3-quart saucepan, then add marshmallows and cook over low heat, stirring constantly until syrupy. Add food colouring and stir until the colour is well mixed in. Remove from heat, add cereal, and stir until well coated. Press into a cookie sheet and let cool. Use metal Christmas-shaped cookie cutters to cut out some Christmas treats.

Smelly Christmas Tree

    Construction paper
    Scissors
    Glue
    One package green Jell-O
    Empty salt shaker or spice container
    Paintbrush
    Hole punch (optional)
    Ribbon or string (optional)

Cut a Christmas tree shape from a piece of construction paper. Use the paintbrush to spread glue all over the tree. Sprinkle Jell-O jelly powder onto the glue. Shake off excess Jell-O and let dry. Use as a Christmas card or picture. If you like, punch a hole in the top of the tree, insert a loop of ribbon or string through the hole, and use as a Christmas tree ornament.

Christmas Bag

Your child can use this bag to "wrap" a gift in, or you can have one on hand for each member of the family on Christmas morning. It will help keep cards and small, opened gifts from getting lost in the sea of boxes, giftwrap, and presents.

Large paper bag
Glue
Bits of wrapping paper, stickers, ribbon, fabric, old Christmas cards

Spread glue on one side of a large paper bag. Let your child stick whatever materials you have handy on the bag: small pieces of holiday wrapping paper, seasonal stickers, ribbon or fabric, or pictures cut from old Christmas cards. If you like, decorate the other side of the bag in the same way.

Gingerbread People

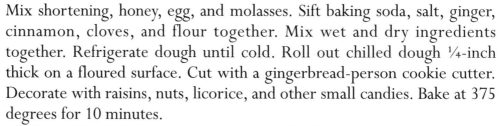

1 cup shortening
¾ cup honey
1 egg
1 cup molasses
1½ teaspoon baking soda
½ teaspoon salt
2 teaspoon ground ginger
1 teaspoon cinnamon
1 teaspoon ground cloves
5 cups flour
Raisins, nuts, licorice, and small candies for decorating

Mix shortening, honey, egg, and molasses. Sift baking soda, salt, ginger, cinnamon, cloves, and flour together. Mix wet and dry ingredients together. Refrigerate dough until cold. Roll out chilled dough ¼-inch thick on a floured surface. Cut with a gingerbread-person cookie cutter. Decorate with raisins, nuts, licorice, and other small candies. Bake at 375 degrees for 10 minutes.

If you like, bake the gingerbread people ahead of time, and let your child decorate the cooled cookies with icing and small candies. If your family members aren't overly fond of gingerbread, don't let that stop you. Substitute another rolled cookie dough recipe instead.

HANUKKAH (Date Varies)

Hanukkah, the most joyous and festive of Jewish holidays, lasts eight days and takes place in December—sometimes early and sometimes late in the month.

Hanukkah, which means "dedication," was first celebrated more than two thousand years ago. Hanukkah commemorates a time when the Holy Temple in Jerusalem had been restored and was about to be rededicated. Only one day's supply of oil for the holy lamps was found, but the lamps miraculously burned for eight days! This is why Hanukkah is also called the Festival of Lights, and why the main focus of the celebration is the lighting of candles. A menorah, a special nine-branch candle holder, is used each day throughout the celebration.

Every year Jews all over the world celebrate Hanukkah. Families gather to light the Hanukkah menorah, remember their ancestors' historic struggle for religious freedom, and recite blessings of thanks to God. Family members exchange gifts, eat special foods, play games, and retell the story of Hanukkah.

Egg Carton Menorah

    Empty egg carton
    Scissors
    Glue, tape, or stapler
    Blue and yellow tempera paint
    Cotton swabs

Divide an egg carton in half (two strips of six sections). Cut three sections from one strip and glue, tape, or staple to the other strip so that you have one strip with nine sections. Paint the nine-section strip blue. Make candles by dipping nine cotton swabs into yellow paint. Poke one through the top of each section.

Older children may enjoy using birthday candles in place of cotton swabs. If you decide to actually light the birthday candles, be sure to supervise carefully. If you find the candles a little loose, secure them by wrapping playdough around the base of the candle where it pokes through the egg carton.

Star of David

Two yellow pipe cleaners or six Popsicle sticks
Glue
Yellow tempera paint (optional)
Paintbrush (optional)
Glitter
Yarn or ribbon

Bend each of two pipe cleaners into a triangle, twisting the ends together securely. If using Popsicle sticks, glue into a triangular shape. Place one triangle upside down on the other. Spread glue at the points where the triangles meet. Let dry. If using Popsicle sticks, paint them yellow if you like. Dab glue onto the star and sprinkle on glitter. Use yarn or ribbon to hang the star from the top of a window or in a doorway.

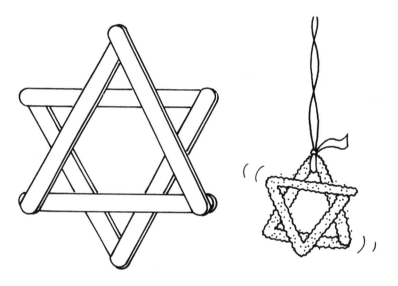

Hanukkah Rubbings

Posterboard or Hanukkah cards with raised Hanukkah symbols
Scissors
Paper
Crayons (paper removed)

Cut Hanukkah symbols from posterboard, or use Hanukkah cards with raised Hanukkah symbols on the front. Place the cutouts on the table, put paper over them, and show your child how to rub a crayon sideways over the paper to create a rubbing of the symbol beneath. Some significant Hanukkah symbols include candles, a menorah, a star of David (six-pointed star), an elephant, and a hammer.

Handprint Menorah

Most one-year-olds will not sit still long enough for this activity, but two- and three-year-olds will enjoy it.

> White, yellow, and orange tempera paint
> Blue construction paper

Paint the palms of your child's hands white (the candleholder), his fingers yellow (the candles), and the tips of his fingers orange (the flames). Cross his hands over and press them onto the blue construction paper (his thumbs will be on opposite ends of the paper). Make sure his pinky fingers overlap as one finger, so the total number of "candles" is nine. You may want to fold the construction paper in half first and use it for a Hanukkah card, or cover it with clear contact paper for a Hanukkah place mat.

Basic Craft Recipes

ALTHOUGH YOUR TODDLER IS STILL QUITE YOUNG, SHE IS ALREADY beginning to develop creative skills. She undoubtedly loves to scribble on paper (or walls) and already may have experienced the joy of fingerpainting. You have probably noticed that she doesn't care as much for what she makes as for the process of working with materials of many different colours and textures. Whether it's the process or the product that interests your child, the craft materials in this appendix are essential for her artwork. On the following pages you'll find easy recipes for paint, glue, paste, modeling compounds, and more.

PAINT

Each of these nine recipes will produce a good-quality paint for your child to use. The ingredients and preparation vary from recipe to recipe, so choose one that best suits the supplies you have on hand and time you have available.

When mixing paint, keep in mind the age of your young artist. As a general rule, younger children require thicker paint and brushes. Paint should always be stored in covered containers. Small plastic spillproof paint containers are available at art-supply stores. Each comes with an airtight lid, holds brushes upright without tipping, and is well worth the purchase price of several dollars.

Flour-Based Poster Paint

¼ cup flour
1 cup water
Powdered tempera paint
Water
Liquid starch or liquid detergent (optional)

Measure flour into a saucepan. Slowly add one cup water to make a smooth paste. Heat, stirring constantly, until mixture begins to thicken. Cool. Measure ¼ cup of the flour paste into small jars or plastic containers. Add 3 tablespoons powdered tempera paint and 2 tablespoons water to each container (use a different colour of paint for each container). For an opaque finish, add liquid starch. For a glossy finish, add liquid detergent. Store covered.

Cornstarch Paint

¾ cup cornstarch
½ cup cold water
4 cups boiling water
Tempera paint

Measure cornstarch into a medium saucepan. Add cold water to cornstarch and stir to make a smooth, thick paste. Stir in boiling water. Place saucepan over low-medium heat and stir until boiling. Boil one minute; remove from heat. Cool. Spoon about ½ cup of the thickened cornstarch mixture into a paint cup or small container, using one paint cup or container for each colour. Stir 1 teaspoon dry tempera paint or 1 tablespoon liquid tempera paint into each cup (use more paint to achieve a deeper, more intense colour). If the paint is too thick, stir in one spoonful of water at a time until the desired consistency is reached. Store in the refrigerator. This recipe makes about 4 cups of paint.

Detergent Poster Paint

1 tablespoon clear liquid detergent
2 teaspoons powdered tempera paint

For each colour, mix together liquid detergent and powdered tempera paint in a small jar or plastic container. This recipe makes enough for one painting session.

Condensed Milk Paint

> 1 cup condensed milk
> Food colouring

Mix one cup of condensed milk in a bowl with a few drops of food colouring to make a very bright, glossy paint. This paint is not intended to be eaten, but it won't harm a child who decides to make a snack of it. Store covered in the refrigerator.

Homemade Face Paint

> 1 teaspoon cornstarch
> ½ teaspoon cold cream
> ½ teaspoon water
> Food colouring

In a bowl, stir together the cornstarch and cold cream until well blended. Add water and stir. Add food colouring one drop at a time until you get the desired colour. Paint designs on face with a small paintbrush; remove with soap and water. Store covered.

Halloween Face Paint

> 1 tablespoon solid shortening
> 2 tablespoons cornstarch
> Food colouring

In a bowl, mix shortening and cornstarch together until smooth. Add food colouring one drop at a time until you get the desired colour. Use a sponge or your fingers to apply paint to a large area, such as an entire face. To apply with a small brush, thin paint with a little water first. Remove with soap and water. Store covered.

Egg Yolk Paint

Use this recipe when you want to paint edible cookies.

> 1 egg yolk
> ¼ teaspoon water
> Food colouring

In a bowl, mix egg yolk with water and lots of food colouring. Use a paint brush to paint on freshly baked cookies; return cookies to oven until paint hardens.

Cornstarch Fingerpaint

> 3 tablespoons sugar
> ½ cup cornstarch
> 2 cups cold water
> Food colouring
> Soap flakes or liquid dishwashing detergent

Mix sugar and cornstarch in a medium saucepan over low heat. Add cold water and stir constantly until the mixture is thick. Remove from heat. Divide the mixture into four or five portions, spooning into muffin-tin section or small cups. Add a few drops of food colouring and a pinch of soap flakes or a drop of liquid dishwashing detergent to each portion. Stir and let cool before using. Store covered in the refrigerator.

Flour Fingerpaint

> 1 cup flour
> 2 tablespoons salt
> 1½ cups cold water
> 1¼ cups hot water
> Food colouring or tempera paint

Put flour and salt in a saucepan. Add cold water and beat with a whisk or rotary beater until smooth. Add hot water and boil until mixture is thick. Beat again until smooth. Colour as desired with food colouring or powdered tempera paint. Store covered in the refrigerator.

PLAYDOUGH

Everyone seems to have their own favourite playdough recipe, and many old favourites have been included here. Some require cooking and some don't; some are meant to be eaten and some are not. Choose the recipe that best suits your needs and the ingredients you have on hand. Store playdough in a covered container or Ziploc bag. If it sweats a little, just add more flour. For sensory variety, warm or chill playdough before using.

Coloured Playdough

> 1 cup water
> 1 tablespoon vegetable oil
> ½ cup salt
> 1 tablespoon cream of tartar
> Food colouring
> 1 cup flour

Combine water, oil, salt, cream of tartar, and a few drops of food colouring in a saucepan and heat until warm. Remove from heat and add flour. Stir, then knead until smooth. Keep in mind that the cream of tartar makes this dough long-lasting—up to six months or longer—so resist the temptation to leave it out if you don't have it on hand. Store this dough in an airtight container or Ziploc bag.

Kool-Aid Playdough

> ½ cup salt
> 2 cups water
> Food colouring, tempera powder, or Kool-Aid for colour
> 2 tablespoons salad oil
> 2 cups sifted flour
> 2 tablespoons alum (available at your grocery or drugstore)

Combine salt and water in a saucepan and boil until salt dissolves. Remove from heat and tint with food colouring, tempera powder, or Kool-Aid. Add salad oil, flour, and alum. Knead until smooth. This dough will last two months or longer.

Uncooked Playdough

1 cup cold water
1 cup salt
2 teaspoons vegetable oil
Tempera paint or food colouring
3 cups flour
2 tablespoons cornstarch

Mix the water, salt, oil, and enough tempera paint or food colouring to make a bright colour. Gradually add flour and cornstarch until the mixtures reaches the consistency of bread dough. Store covered.

Salt Playdough

1 cup salt
1 cup water
½ cup flour plus additional flour

Mix salt, water, and flour in a saucepan and cook over medium heat. Remove from heat when mixture is thick and rubbery. As the mixture cools, knead in enough flour to make the dough workable.

Oatmeal Playdough

1 part flour
1 part water
2 parts oatmeal

Combine all ingredients in a bowl; mix well and knead until smooth. This playdough is not intended to be eaten, but it will not hurt a child who decides to taste it. Store covered in the refrigerator. Your child may be able to make this playdough with very little help from you, but it doesn't last as long as cooked playdough.

Peanut Butter Playdough

2 cups peanut butter
6 tablespoons honey

Non-fat dry milk or milk plus flour
Cocoa or carob for chocolate flavour (optional)
Edible treats for decoration

Combine all ingredients in a bowl and mix, adding enough dry milk or milk plus flour to reach the consistency of bread dough. Add cocoa or carob, if desired. Shape, decorate with other edible treats, and eat!

CLAY

Use the following recipes to make clay that can be rolled or shaped into sculptures. The drying methods vary, either overnight or in the oven. When hard, ornaments can be painted and preserved with acrylic.

No-Bake Craft Clay

1 cup cornstarch
1¼ cups cold water
2 cups baking soda (500 grams or 1 pound)
Food colouring (optional)
Tempera or acrylic paints (optional)

Combine cornstarch, water, and baking soda in a saucepan; stir over medium heat for about 4 minutes until the mixture thickens to a moist mashed-potato consistency. (For coloured clay, add a few drops of food colouring to the water before it is mixed with cornstarch and baking soda.) Remove from heat, turn onto a plate and cover with a damp cloth until cool. Knead until smooth. Shape as desired or store in an airtight container or Ziploc bag. Dry sculptures overnight, then paint with tempera or acrylic. Dip in shellac, spray with clear acrylic, or brush with clear nail polish to seal.

Modeling Clay

2 cups salt
Water
1 cup cornstarch

Stir salt and ⅔ cup water in a saucepan over heat four to five minutes. Remove from heat; add cornstarch and ½ cup cold water. Stir until smooth; return to heat and cook until thick. Allow mixture to cool, then shape as desired. When dry, decorate with paint, markers, glitter, and so on. Finish with clear acrylic spray or clear nail polish. Store in a Ziploc bag.

No-Bake Cookie Clay

> 2 cups salt
> Water
> 1 cup cornstarch
> Paint, glitter, and other decorative materials

Mix salt with ⅔ cup water in a medium saucepan. Stir and boil until salt dissolves. Remove from heat. Add cornstarch and ½ cup cold water and stir. If the mixture doesn't immediately thicken, heat and stir until it does. Sprinkle cornstarch on table and rolling pin. Roll out the dough with the rolling pin and cut with cookie cutters. Use a straw to make a hole for hanging. Let dry overnight and decorate with paint, glitter, and so on. These ornaments are not edible.

Baker's Clay

> 4 cups flour
> 1 cup salt
> 1 teaspoon powdered alum
> 1½ cups water
> Food colouring (optional)

Mix flour, salt, alum, and water in a large bowl. If the dough is too dry, work in another tablespoon of water. Dough can be coloured by dividing it into several parts and kneading a few drops of food colouring into each part. Roll or mould as desired.

To Roll: Roll dough ⅛-inch thick on a lightly floured surface. Cut with cookie cutters dipped in flour. Make a hole for hanging by dipping the end of a drinking straw in flour and using the straw to cut a tiny circle ¼-inch from the ornament's edge. If you like, shake the dots of clay from the straw and press on as decorations.

To Mould: Shape dough into figures such as flowers, fruits, animals, and so on. The figures should be no more than ½-inch thick.

Insert a fine wire in ornaments for hanging. Bake ornaments on an ungreased cookie sheet for about 30 minutes in a 250 degree oven. Turn and bake another 90 minutes until hard and dry. Remove and cool, then smooth with fine sandpaper. Paint both sides of the ornament with plastic-based poster paint, acrylic paint, or markers. Let dry and seal with clear shellac, acrylic spray, or clear nail polish.

Makes about five dozen 2½-inch ornaments.

Bread Clay

6 slices white bread, crusts removed
6 tablespoons white glue
½ teaspoon detergent or 2 teaspoons glycerine
Food colouring

Knead bread with glue plus detergent or glycerine until the mixture is no longer sticky. Separate into portions and tint with food colouring. Let your child shape the clay. Brush the sculpture with equal parts glue and water for a smooth appearance. Let dry overnight to harden. Use acrylic paints, acrylic spray, or clear nail polish to seal and preserve.

GLUE & PASTE

The following glue and paste recipes use a variety of ingredients and methods. Choose the one that best suits your project. For variety, add food colouring to glue before using. Store all products in an airtight container in the refrigerator.

Glue

Water
2 tablespoons corn syrup
1 teaspoon white vinegar
2 tablespoons cornstarch

Mix ¾ cup water, corn syrup, and white vinegar in a small saucepan. Bring to a full rolling boil. In a small bowl, mix cornstarch with ¾ cup cold water. Add this mixture slowly to the hot mixture, stirring constantly until the mixture returns to a boil. Boil for one minute, then remove from heat. When slightly cooled, pour into another container and let stand overnight before using.

Homemade Paste

½ cup flour
Cold water
Food colouring (optional)

Measure flour into a saucepan. Add water to the flour until it is as thick as cream. Simmer, stirring constantly, for five minutes. Remove from heat. Add a few drops of food colouring, if desired. Allow to cool before using. This makes a wet, messy paste that takes a while to dry.

Papier-Mâché Paste

1 cup water
¼ cup flour
5 cups lightly boiling water

Lightly boil 5 cups of water in a saucepan. Measure flour into a small bowl. Add 1 cup of water (the mixture will be thin and runny). Stir this mixture into the lightly boiling water. Gently boil and stir for two to three minutes. Cool before using.

No-Cook Paste

½ cup flour
Water
Salt

Mix the flour with water until gooey. Add a pinch of salt; stir.

OTHER CRAFT RECIPES

Use the following recipes to make interesting materials for use in various art and craft projects.

Pasta and Rice Dye

½ cup rubbing alcohol
Food colouring
Uncooked pasta or rice

Mix alcohol and food colouring in a bowl. Add small amounts of rice or dry pasta to the liquid and gently mix. The larger the pasta, the longer it will take to absorb the colour. Dry the dyed pasta or rice on newspapers covered with wax paper.

Egg Dye

¼ teaspoon food colouring
¼ cup hot water
1 tablespoon white vinegar

Measure food colouring, hot water, and vinegar into a bowl or a cup and mix. Use different food colouring in each container for desired shades. Soak eggs in the dyes until they reach the desired shades.

Ornamental Frosting

This frosting works like an edible glue; use for gingerbread houses or other food projects that you want to eat.

3 egg whites
1 teaspoon cream of tartar
500 grams (1 pound) sifted icing sugar (about 4 cups)

Beat egg whites with cream of tartar in a bowl until stiff peaks form. Add sifted icing sugar and continue beating until mixture is thick and holds its shape. Cover with a damp cloth when not in use. This can be made several hours or the day before using. Store in an airtight container in the refrigerator.

Colourful Creative Salt

½ cup salt
5 to 6 drops food colouring

Add food colouring to salt and stir well. Cook in a microwave for one to two minutes, or spread on wax paper and let air dry. Store in an airtight container. Use as you would glitter.

Crazy Can Activities

THE FOLLOWING ACTIVITIES ARE SUITABLE FOR A TODDLER CRAZY CAN (see Chapter 1). These activities are suggested because they require no special materials, need no time-consuming preparation or cleanup, and above all, demand a minimal amount of adult participation. Some of these ideas require a little advance planning, for instance have a collection of nuts and bolts on hand for the Nuts and Bolts activity, or prepare a craft carton for Cartons of Fun. These activities will provide you with an instant remedy when things start to get crazy, or when there's just "nothing to do." (The number following each activity refers to the page number on which that activity is found.)

Bottles and Lids   20
Cartons of Fun   34
Chair Maze   31
Clothespin Can   27
Clothespin Drop   26
Clothespin Poke   26
Felt Faces   92
Fun with Balls   43
Fun with Kleenex   32
Fun with Tape   21
Ice Cube Bags   20
Jingle Bell Bracelet   125
Magic Painting   145
Mail Box   25

No-Cook Squishy Bag   40
Nuts and Bolts   27
Painting Bag   40
Porcupine Playdough   32
Ring Fun   24
Sandpaper Play   90
Stacking Fun   45
Sticky Feet   29
Threading   24

Best Toys for Babies and Toddlers

IF YOUR CHILD HAS NOT YET REACHED HER FIRST BIRTHDAY, CHANCES ARE she has not yet amassed a great collection of toys. After a few birthdays and Christmas celebrations, however, she will likely have more toys than you ever dreamed possible! If that has not yet happened, it's a good idea to think about the kind of toys you want yourself and others to invest in. There are a lot of great toys out there for kids, and more coming out all the time. Some are worth the money that is spent, while others definitely aren't.

When choosing toys for children, try to look for items that can be used in more than one way, toys that have stood the test of time, and those that can be played with through many years of childhood. The toys listed in this appendix meet all those criteria, and are sure to be worth every penny spent on them.

When storing toys, try to stay away from toy boxes. We have two, lovingly hand-made by Grandpa, which we now use for stuffed animals and dress-up clothes. Other items with many pieces are stored in see-through, stackable, plastic containers with lids. These stack up well in children's closets, or on wooden shelving in the playroom. Flat containers also slide easily under children's beds, utilizing otherwise unused space. Storing toys in this way helps keep the toys organized, keeps pieces of toys from getting mixed up with each other (provided you don't allow your child to take all the containers out at once), and helps children develop organizational skills.

Other ideas for making the best use of toys include establishing a toy rotation or implementing a toy exchange with friends. See Chapter 1 for further details.

When reading *What to Expect the Toddler Years* (Arlene Eisenberg, Heidi E. Markoff, Sandee E. Hathaway, Workman Publishing, NY, 1994), I came across a great list called "Toys for Tots Early in the Second Year." Most of our family favourites were included in the list, but I liked the way the list was organized according to the skill each particular toy helps to develop. I have organized the following list in somewhat the same way. Many of the toys help to develop more than one type of skill, but for the sake of simplicity, I haven't duplicated these in each category.

Toys that help build small-motor skills

(Many of these items also encourage discovery and interest in the physical world.) Nesting and stacking toys; simple wooden jigsaw puzzles; shape-sorters; blocks; boxes and containers for filling and emptying; beads or spools to string (for olders toddlers); sandbox and sandbox toys; waterplay toys.

Toys that help build large-motor skills

Pull along toys; push toys; riding toys; swings and slides; balls of all sizes.

Toys that stimulate imagination

(Many of these toys also encourage learning about the grown-up world.) Stuffed animals; dolls; doll furniture and accessories; fake food; tea set; kitchen accessories; shopping cart; toy cars, trucks, and so on; toy telephone; dress-up clothes and accessories; building toys (Lego, Duplo); books; puppets.

Toys that stimulate creativity

(I call these basic craft supplies.) Crayons; paper; colouring books; markers; paint; brushes; sponges; playdough; glue; child-safe scissors.

Toys that encourage musical play

Drums; tambourines; maracas; xylophones; simple keyboards; sturdy cassette player and tapes.

Best Books for Babies and Toddlers

THIS LIST OF OVER 70 AUTHORS AND THEIR BOOKS IS IN NO WAY complete. Each author may have written many titles, of which only one or two are included here. Many great children's authors and books have not been included, not because they are not worthy, but because to include them all would require another book entirely! This list includes some of the books and authors that are recommended by "experts" in the field of children's literature, many of which our family has read and enjoyed over the years.

The best way to know what books your child will enjoy is to read children's books—lots of them. Read award-winners and award-losers (some of the best-loved books are runners-up or "losers!"). Read books about children's books, too. My favourite books about books, ones that I have relied on for many years, include *Honey for a Child's Heart,* by Gladys Hunt, *The Read-Aloud Handbook,* by Jim Trelease, and *Reading for the Love of It,* by Michele Landsberg. Publication information for these titles is listed in Appendix E.

Make the children's room of your library your second home. Get to know the librarians, and ask for recommendations. The most popular books are usually checked out as soon as they are returned, so reserve if you can. If you have access to a computer, you can often reserve books from home—a life-saver for those who visit the library with infants and toddlers! Failing this, schedule an afternoon or evening to visit the library without toddlers in tow, and spend some time familiarizing yourself with the best in children's books, both old and new.

Ahlberg, Janet
  Baby's Catalogue
  Peek-A-Boo

Bang, Molly
  Ten, Nine, Eight
  Yellow Ball

Becker, Bonny
  The Quiet Way Home

Brown, Margaret Wise
  Goodnight Moon
  The Big Red Barn
  The Runaway Bunny

Bruna, Dick
  Dick Bruna's Animal Book
  I Can Count
  I Can Dress Myself
  Miffy series
  My Shirt is White

Burningham, John
  Mr. Gumpy's Outing

Carle, Eric
  My Very First Book of Colors
  The Very Busy Spider
  The Very Hungry Caterpillar

Carlstrom, Nancy W.
  Jesse Bear, What Will You Wear?

Carter, Noelle and David
  I'm a Little Mouse

Cooke, Trish
  So Much

Cooney, Barbara
  Chanticleer and the Fox

Cousins, Lucy (illustrator)
  The Little Dog Laughed and other Nursery Rhymes from Mother Goose

Crews, Donald
  Freight Train
  Truck

deAngeli, Marguerite
  Book of Nursery and Mother Goose Rhymes

dePaola, Tomi
  Charlie Needs a Cloak
  Pancakes for Breakfast

deRegniers, Beatrice Schenk
  May I Bring a Friend?

Demarest, Chris L.
  My Blue Boat

Dunn, Judy
  The Little Rabbit

Eastman, P.D.
  Are You My Mother?

Eichenberg, Fritz
  Ape in a Cape: An Alphabet of Odd Animals
  Dancing in the Moon

Ets, Marie Hall
  In the Forest
  Gilberto and the Wind
  Play With Me

Flack, Marjorie
  Angus series
  Ask Mister Bear
  Walter, the Lazy Mouse

Freeman, Don
  Corduroy
  The Chalk Box Story

Fujikawa, Gyo
  Let's Eat
  Puppies, Pussy Cats and Other Friends

Gág, Wanda
  The ABC Bunny

Galdone, Paul
  Old Woman and Her Pig
  Old Mother Hubbard and Her Dog
  The Monkey and the Crocodile
  The Little Red Hen

Gilham, Bill
  The First Words Picture Book

Goudey, Alice
  The Day We Saw the Sun Come Up

Gramatky, Hardie
  Little Toot

Greenaway, Kate
  A Apple Pie

Hill, Eric
  Spot series

Hoban, Tana
  Circles, Triangles, and Squares

Is It Red? Is It Yellow? Is It Blue?
Push Pull, Empty Full

Hughes, Shirley
  Bathwater's Hot
  Noisy
  Two Shoes, New Shoes
  When We Went to the Park

Jam, Teddy
  Night Cars

Johnson, Crockett
  Harold and the Purple Crayon

Keats, Ezra Jacks
  Peter's Chair
  The Snowy Day

Kraus, Robert
  Whose Mouse Are You?

Krauss, Ruth
  A Hole is to Dig: A First Book of First Definitions
  Bears
  The Bundle Book
  The Carrot Book
  The Happy Day

Lansky, Bruce
  The New Adventures of Mother Goose

Lionni, Leo
  Frederick
  Fish is Fish
  Swimmy

Martin, Bill
  Brown Bear, Brown Bear, What Do You See?
  Chicka Chicka Boom Boom

McCloskey, Robert
  Blueberries for Sal

McMillan, Bruce
  Here a Chick, There a Chick

Ormerod, Jan
  101 Things To Do With a Baby

Oxenbury, Helen
  Helen Oxenbury's ABC of Things
  Tom and Pippo series

Parish, Peggy
  I Can! Can You?

Payne, Emmy
  Katy No-Pocket

Pienkowski, Jan
  ABC
  Colors
  Numbers
  Shapes

Piper, Watty
  The Little Engine That Could

Potter, Beatrix
  The Complete Adventures of Peter Rabbit

Ransom, Candice
  The Big Green Pocketbook

Reid, Barbara
  Zoe series

Rey, H.A.
  Curious George

Rockwell, Anne
  Come to Town

Rosen, Michael
  We're Going on a Bear Hunt

Scarry, Richard
  Best Word Book
  Cars and Trucks and Things That Go
  Please and Thank You Book
  The Early Bird

Sendak, Maurice
  Alligators All Around

Slobodkina, Esphyr
  Caps for Sale

Spier, Peter
  Big Trucks, Little Trucks
  Fast Cars, Slow Cars
  Fast-Slow High-Low
  Here Comes the Fire Trucks
  Noah's Ark
  Trucks that Dig and Dump

Tafuri, Nancy
  Early Morning in the Barn
  Have You Seen My Duckling?
  One Wet Jacket
  Two New Sneakers

Tresselt, Alvin
White Snow, Bright Snow

Tudor, Tasha
A Is for Annabelle

Waddell, Martin
Owl Babies

Wells, Rosemary
Max series

Wildsmith, Brian
Brian Wildsmith's Wild Animals
Brian Wildsmith's 1, 2, 3's

Williams, Garth
Chicken Book

Williams, Vera
"More, More, More," Said the Baby

Wood, Audrey
The Napping House

Zion, Gene
Harry the Dirty Dog

Zolotow, Charlotte
Big Sister and Little Sister
Some Things Go Together
The Sleepy Book
William's Doll

Resources

VERY FEW IDEAS IN THIS WORLD ARE TRULY ORIGINAL—SOMEONE, somewhere, has probably had that same idea before. Many of the ideas in this book have appeared in print elsewhere, and many you have probably seen, heard about, or done yourself. I have tried to include in this book only the very best ideas for toddlers, the ones that are the most fun, as well as the ones that are the most practical for parents and caregivers to manage. The ideas were gleaned from a combination of personal experience, contributions from friends and family, and ideas and information gathered from the books listed below.

Baby Games, Elaine Martin,
   Stoddart Publishing, Toronto, ON, 1988

Creative Activities for Young Children, 4th Edition, Mary Mayesky,
   Delmar Publishers Inc., Albany, NY, 1990

Do Touch: Instant, Easy Hands-On Learning Experiences for Young Chidren,
   Labritta Gilbert, Gryphon House, Beltsville, MD, 1989

Earth-Friendly Toys, George Pfiffners
   John Wiley and Sons, Inc., 1994

Feed Me! I'm Yours, Vicky Lansky,
   Meadowbrook Press, 1974

Games for the Very Young, Elizabeth Matterson
   American Heritage Press, New York, NY, 1969

Games to Play with Toddlers, Jackie Silberg,
Gryphon House, Beltsville, MD, 1993

Games to Play with Two Year Olds, Jackie Silberg,
Gryphon House, Beltsville, MD, 1994

Giant Encyclopedia of Theme Activities for Children 2 to 5, The,
edited by Kathy Charner, Gryphon House, Beltsville, MD, 1993

Joyful Play with Toddlers, Sandi Dexter,
Parenting Press, Inc., Seattle, WA, 1995

Holiday Crafts, Anna Suid,
Monday Morning Books, 1985

Honey for a Child's Heart, 3rd Edition, Gladys Hunt,
Zondervan Books, Grand Rapids, MI, 1989

Look at Me: Creative Learning Activities for Babies and Toddlers,
Carolyn Buhai Haas, Chicago Review Press, 1987

More Things to Do with Toddlers and Twos, Karen Miller,
TelShare Publishing, Chelsea, MA 1990

150 Plus! Games and Activities for Early Childhood, Zane Spencer,
Fearon Publishers Inc., Belmont, CA, 1976

1-2-3 Art, Jean Warren,
Warren Publishing House, Everett, WA, 1985

Parents are Teachers, Too, Claudia Jones,
Williamson Publishing Co., Charlotte, Vermont, 1988

Preschool Art, Mary Ann Kohl,
Gryphon House, Beltsville, MD, 1994

Preparing Young Children for Math, Claudia Zaslavsky,
Schocken Books, NY, 1979

Read-Aloud Handbook, The, 4th Edition, Jim Trelease,
Penguin Books, NY, 1995

Read to Me! Teach Me!, Mary Jane Mangini Rossi,
    American Baby Books, Wauwatosa, WI, 1982

Reading for the Love of It, Michele Landsberg,
    Prentice Hall Press, 1987

Things to Do with Toddlers and Twos, Karen Miller,
    Telshare Publishing, Chelsea, MA, 1984

365 Days of Baby Love, Sheila Ellison and Judith Gray,
    Sourcebooks, Inc., Naperville, IL, 1996

365 Days of Creative Play, Sheila Ellison and Judith Gray,
    Sourcebooks, Inc., Naperville, IL, 1995

365 Foods Kids Love to Eat, Sheila Ellison and Judith Gray,
    Sourcebooks, Inc, Naperville, IL, 1995

Toddlers Together: The Complete Planning Guide for a Toddler Curriculum,
    Cynthia Catlin, Gryphon House, Beltsville, MD, 1994

Understanding Your Child Through Play, Maggie Jones,
    Stoddart Publishing, Toronto, ON, 1989

What to Expect the Toddler Years, Arlene Eisenberg, Heidi E. Markoff,
    Sandee E. Hathaway, Workman Publishing, NY, 1994

Wonderplay, Fretta Reitzes and Beth Teitelman,
    Running Press, Philadelphia, PA, 1995

Your Baby & Child From Birth to Age Five, Penelope Leach,
    Alfred A. Knopf, New York, NY, 1990

The United States General Services Administration makes available many free and low-cost federal publications of consumer interest, including many on learning activities and parenting. For a free catalog write to:

    Consumer Information Centre-2C
    P.O. Box 100
    Pueblo, Colorado 81002

A

All Gone!, 28
Alphabet Sand, 115
Animal Dress-Up, 190
Animal Sort, 105
Ants on a Log, 60
Appendices, 199
Apple Seed Count, 120
Apple Shake-Ups, 63
Apple Smiles, 58
Arts and Crafts, 131
Artwork Display, 164
Ask a Question, 88

B

Baker's Box, 6
Baker's Clay, 206
Ball Splash, 75
Balloon Fun, 46
Balloon Kites, 82
Balloon Play, 46
Balls, Balls, Balls, 43
Bananas, Honey, and Wheat Germ, 57
Basic Craft Recipes, 199
Baster Play, 73
Bathtime Bubbles, 69
Bathtub Fingerpainting, 151
Bathtub Soap Paint, 70
Beanbag Crawl, 47
Beanbag Races, 47
Beanbag Toss, 115
Beanbag Throw, 48
Bear in the Basket, 30
Bedtime Buddy, 167
Berry Basket Printing, 153
Best Books for Babies and Toddlers, 214
Best Toys for Babies and Toddlers, 212
Big Mouth Game, 50
Birthday Celebrations, 170
Birthday Memory Book, 171
Blanket Riding, 33

Block Printing, 154
Block Sorter, 23
Book Mark, 165
Bottles and Lids, 20
Bread Clay, 207
Bubble Bottle, 25
Bubble Fun, 81
Bubble Solution, 80
Bubble Wrap Printing, 153
Busy Bag, 9
Busy Box, 6
Butterfly Sandwiches, 56
Button Tap, 122

C

Can You Find Your Knee?, 103
Canada Day, 181
Canada Day Salad, 182
Car Book, 89
Car Wash, 73
Cardboard Printing, 153
Cars and Colours, 110
Cartons of Fun, 34
Cereal Box Puzzles, 35
Chair Maze, 31
Chalk Fun, 136
Changing Colours, 85
Christmas, 187
Christmas Bag, 193
Christmas Doorknob Decoration, 191
Christmas Noisemaker, 189
Christmas Shapes, 192
Christmas Tree, 191
Cinnamon Drawing, 191
Clay, 205
Climbing Practice, 128
Cling Wrap Painting, 146
Clothespin Can, 27
Clothespin Colours, 110
Clothespin Drop, 26
Clothespin Poke, 26

Coffee Can Drum, 122
Colour Cards, 109
Colour Cube, 113
Colour Game, 107
Colour Hunt, 111
Colour Match, 109
Colour of the Day, 88
Coloured Ice Cubes, 71
Coloured Playdough, 203
Coloured Sand, 75
Colourful Clothespins, 111
Colourful Creative Salt, 210
Condensed Milk Paint, 201
Cork Printing, 155
Cork Race, 67
Corn Cob Painting, 149
Cornstarch Fingerpaint, 202
Cornstarch Paint, 200
Cottonball Snowman, 189
Crafts and Other Fun
    Things to Make, 163
Crayon Slide, 85
Crazy Can, 9
Crazy Can Activities, 211
Crumple Painting, 143
Cylinder Pictures, 137

D

Dance and Fall Down, 127
Dance Ribbon, 126
Dancing with Scarves, 127
Detergent Poster Paint, 200
Digging for Treasure, 84
Dodge Ball, 81
Doll Bed, 17
Drawing, 133
Drown the Penny, 69
Dry Leaf Collage, 183
Dry Painting, 142
Dump Cake, 57
Duplo Printing, 155

E

Early Learning Fun, 101
Early Morning Fun, 38
Easter, 178
Easter Bouquet, 179
Easter Egg Holder, 178
Easter Egg Maracas, 126
Easter Egg Necklace, 180
Easter Egg Pick-Up, 180
Easy Bird Feeder, 37
Easy Easter Eggs, 178
Edible Valentines, 174
Egg Carton Menorah, 195
Egg Dye, 209
Egg Sort, 106
Egg Yolk Paint, 202
Encouragement, 14

F

Face Paint, 201
Feather Painting, 146
Feather Printing, 184
Felt Faces, 91
Find Mr. Different, 117
Find the Colour, 109
Finger Plays, 93
Fingerpainting, 150
Fireworks Printing, 181
Fishy Beanbag, 165
Fishy Necklace, 166
Five Little Mice, 99
Five Little Monkeys, 100
Flag Snacks, 182
Flashlight Fun, 21
Flour Fingerpaint, 202
Flour-Based Poster Paint, 200
Fly Swatter Painting, 141
Flying Fish, 38
Follow the Leader, 128
Food Colouring Fingerpaint, 151
Food Colouring Painting, 141

Foot Tracing, 135
Footprint T-Shirt, 166
Frog in the Grass, 79
Frosty Snow Painting, 148
Fruit Dips, 56
Fruit Loop Sand, 157
Fruit Popsicles, 59
Fruit Salad, 60
Fun with Balls, 43
Fun with Kleenex, 32
Fun with Tape, 21
Fun with Water, 67
Funnels and Tubes, 76

G

Giftwrap Collage, 157
Gingerbread People, 194
Glitter Shapes, 160
Glue, 207
Glue and Paste, 207
Glue Printing, 152
Gluing, 156
Gone Fishing, 74
Grandmother's Glasses, 96
Grocery Store, 29

H

Halloween, 185
Halloween Face Paint, 201
Handprint Menorah, 197
Hanukkah, 195
Hanukkah Rubbings, 196
Happy Days, 95
Help! I Have a Toddler!, 3
Here's a Ball for Baby, 97
Hide the Beanbag, 48
Highchair Fun, 22
Holiday Activities, 169
Homemade Butter, 55
Homemade Face Paint, 201
Homemade Paste, 208

I

I Hear Thunder, 97
I Think I Can, 37
I Touch My Head, 95
Ice Blocks, 71
Ice Cube Bags, 20
Ice Cube Painting, 144
Ice Play, 73
Ice Popsicle Painting, 143
Indoor Baseball, 48
Indoor Sandbox, 28
Inside/Outside Voice, 16
Interrupt Rule, 36

J

Jack-O-Orange, 187
Jell-O Jumping, 79
Jell-O Painting, 173
Jell-O Paints, 56
Jingle Bell Bracelet, 125
Jingle Bell Roller, 125
Job Jar, 8
Jungle Safari, 32

K

Kazoo, 123
Kids in the Kitchen, 53
Kool-Aid Playdough, 203
Krispie Christmas Treats, 193

L

Large and Small, 105
Leaf Scrunch, 77
Let's Pretend, 128
Letter Sandwiches, 54
Little Pussy Cats, 97

M

Magic Mud, 39
Magic Painting, 145
Mail Box, 25

Mailman, 113
Maple Leaf Sponge Painting, 181
Marching Song, 99
Marker Drawing, 135
Marker Painting, 142
Marshmallow Treats, 61
Measuring Magic, 78
Memory, 107
Michelangelo's Bathroom, 68
Mini Mask, 36
Mini Olympics, 50
Mirror Play, 129
Mix a Pancake, 96
Modeling Clay, 205
Monkey, Monkey!, 32
More Balloon Fun, 47
More Pompom Fun, 106
Mud Balls, 59
Mud Handprints, 78
Muffin Tin Printing, 154
Music and Movement, 121
Musical Animals, 51

N

Napkin Bug, 34
Nature Bracelet, 79
Nesting Cans, 31
Net Ball, 42
No-Bake Banana Cookies, 59
No-Bake Cookie Clay, 206
No-Bake Craft Clay, 205
No-Cook Paste, 208
No-Cook Squishy Bag, 40
Number Cube, 119
Nursery Rhyme Fun, 89
Nursery Rhymes, 93
Nursing Basket, 35
Nuts and Bolts, 27

O

Oatmeal Playdough, 204

Object Match-Up, 116
Obstacle Course, 49
Organizing for a Toddler, 5
Ornamental Frosting, 209
Out and About, 87
Outdoor Adventures, 77

P

Paint, 199
Paint Dancing, 150
Paint Pen, 147
Paint Popsicles, 144
Paint with Water, 143
Painted Place Mats, 145
Painted Spider's Web, 186
Painted Toast, 63
Painting, 138
Painting Bag, 40
Paper Bag Blocks, 45
Paper Bag Faces, 159
Paper Bag Pumpkin, 186
Paper Bag Shaker, 124
Paper Plate Numbers, 118
Paper Plate Spider's Web, 187
Paper Towel Drawing, 138
Papier-Mâché Paste, 208
Parking Game, 112
Party Tablecloth, 172
Pasta and Rice Dye, 209
Pasta Sort, 106
Paste, 207
Pathfinding, 161
Peanut Butter Playdough, 204
Peanut Butter Sculptures, 61
Pencil Holder, 188
People Blocks, 44
People Puppets, 37
Picture Box, 102
Picture Menus, 55
Picture Sort, 103
Pictures, Pictures, 104

Pipe Play, 41
Planning Your Activities, 10
Playdough, 203
Playdough Numbers, 118
Pocket Matching, 108
Pompom Fun, 104
Popcorn Picture, 158
Porcupine Playdough, 32
Potato Press Picture, 176
Potty Pals, 35
Practical Math, 117
Printmaking, 152
Pudding Cookies, 62
Pudding Paints, 55
Pull Box, 30
Pumpkin Prints, 185

Q
Quickie Cookies, 62

R
Rainbow Crayons, 134
Rainbow Painting, 147
Rainbow Turkey, 183
Rainy Day Box, 8
Rainy Day Play, 15
Red, Red, Red, 79
Resources, 219
Rice Dye, 209
Ring Fun, 24
Rock Drop, 71
Rock Painting, 149
Rock Play, 27
Rope Games, 84
Round and Round the Garden, 95
Row, Row, Row Your Boat, 127
Rudolph Sandwiches, 190

S
Salad Spinner Art, 147
Salt Pictures, 159
Salt Playdough, 204

Sandpaper Play, 90
Scribbling and Drawing, 133
Search and Sort, 111
Shadow Tracing, 83
Shaker Bottle, 19
Shamrock Necklace, 177
Shamrock Rubbings, 177
Shape Match-Up, 115
Shaving Cream Fingerpaint, 151
Sheet Day, 18
Sheet Painting, 140
Shopping List, 90
Short and Tall, 105
Simple Shaker, 124
Simple Sorter, 23
Slowly, Slowly, 94
Smelly Christmas Tree, 193
Snow Painting, 85
Snowflakes, 99
Soap Crayons, 68
Sock Match-Up, 120
Spaghetti Mobiles, 162
Spaghetti Splash, 82
Sponge Blocks, 44
Sponge Play, 70
Sponge Printing, 156
Sponge Tag, 75
Spool Printing, 155
Spoon Match-Up, 105
Squeeze Painting, 145
Squishy Bag, 40
St. Patrick's Day, 176
Stacking Fun, 45
Star of David, 196
Sticker Art, 164
Sticky Feet, 29
Sticky Figures, 19
Stocking Your Craft Cupboard, 11
Stone Paperweight, 192
Stop!, 127
Stop and Go, 91
Straw Painting, 141

String Painting, 148
Strumming Fun, 123
Surprise Tins, 20
Sweetheart Sandwiches, 175

T

Take-Along Tape, 92
Tape City, 17
Tape Collage, 160
Tape Shapes, 116
Target Practice, 74
Tearing, Gluing, and Sticking, 156
Teddy Swing, 83
Ten Little Gentlemen, 94
Texture Touch, 18
Thanksgiving, 182
Thanksgiving Place Mat, 183
Thanksgiving Turkey, 184
Things to Buy, 12
Things to Save, 11
Threading, 24
Tickle Trunk, 7
Tiny Tambourine, 124
Tissue Easter Egg, 180
Tissue Paper Collage, 159
Tissue Paper Eggs, 179
Toddler Ball, 81
Toddler Blocks, 44
Toddler Bowling, 48
Toddler Brag Book, 92
Toddler Collage, 163
Toddler Gymnastics, 129
Toddler Mural, 137
Toddler Obstacle Course, 49
Toddler Pouch, 39
Toddler Sprinkler, 72
Toddler Train, 33
Toddler Trampoline, 128
Toddler Triangle, 124
Toy Car Printing, 155
Toy Rotation, 8
Tube Ball, 42

Tube Fun, 41
Tubes and Balls, 42
Turntable Fun, 114
Two Little Eyes, 94

U

Uncooked Playdough, 204
Unwrapping Game, 18

V

Valentine Cookies, 173
Valentine Cupcakes, 175
Valentine Hearts, 175
Valentine Postcard, 174
Valentine's Day, 173
Vegetable Teethers, 58
Video Time Capsule, 172

W

Walking Through the Jungle, 98
Wash the Floor, 66
Washing Vegetables, 61
Water Balloon Catch, 76
Water Play, 65, 70
Water Rhythms, 72
Waterfall Game, 68
Wave Bottle, 25
Waxed Paper Art, 161
Wet the Chalkboard, 75
What About Television?, 13
What Is It?, 58
What Would Happen If…?, 87
What Would You Be?, 88
What's in the Jar?, 29
Where Is It?, 88
Where's Teddy?, 31
Who Do You See?, 21
Window Painting, 85

Z

Zoo Sandwiches, 64

About the Author

Trish Kuffner lives with her husband, Wayne, and five children, Andria, Emily, Joshua, Johanna, and Samuel, on an acreage in Coquitlam, just outside of Vancouver, B.C. After the birth of her second child in 1990, Trish left a demanding computer programing position to join the growing number of women choosing full-time motherhood over career.

Since the publication of her first book, *Surviving Your Preschooler,* in 1992, Trish has spoken to many parent and caregiver groups in British Columbia and Washington. She enjoys being a source of encouragement to others, and gives all the praise and glory to God for His unfailing love, mercy, grace, and leading in her life.

Trish is currently writing her third book, *Picture Book Activities for Preschoolers,* to be published in Canada and the United States by Meadowbrook Press in the fall of 2000. Trish and Wayne homeschool their five chidlren.

If you've enjoyed *Surviving Your Toddler*, don't miss *Surviving Your Preschooler*, the National Bestseller by Trish Kuffner.

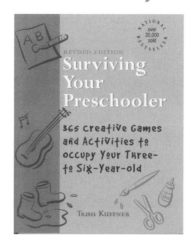

Since *Surviving Your Preschooler* was first published in 1992, it has sold more than 25,000 copies in Canada alone. In 1998 it was published in the United States as *The Preschooler's Busy Book* by Meadowbrook Press. It has also been published in Korean, with further foreign translations in the works.

Surviving Your Preschooler contains 365 activities for three- to six-year-olds using things found around the home. In a format similar to *Surviving Your Toddler, Surviving Your Preschooler* shows parents and day-care providers:

- ◀ How to prevent boredom during even the longest stretches of indoor weather with ideas for indoor play, kitchen activities, and arts and crafts projects.
- ▶ How to stimulate a child's natural curiosity about our world with fun reading, math, and science activities.
- ◀ How to encourage a child's physical, mental, and emotional growth with ideas for music, dance, drama, and outdoor play.
- ▼ How to celebrate holidays and other occasions with special projects and activities.
- ▶ How to keep children occupied during long trips or cross-town errands.

Trish Kuffner writes with the warmth and understanding of a mother who has been there. If you are raising or caring for a preschool-age child, this is one book you won't want to miss! *Surviving Your Preschooler* is available at bookstores across the country, or use the handy order form at the back of this book to order a copy by mail.

Use this convenient order form
to order *Surviving Your Preschooler*
or additional copies of *Surviving Your Toddler*.

Surviving Your Toddler and *Surviving Your Preschooler* make wonderful gifts for family and friends with young children. These books are available in many fine bookstores across the country. We appreciate the support these stores have given us, and encourage you to patronize them. But if your local stores aren't carrying *Surviving Your Toddler* or *Surviving Your Preschooler*, we'd be happy to fill your mail order. Just complete the form below.

Special discounts are available to those who purchase in bulk, making *Surviving Your Toddler* and *Surviving Your Preschooler* natural fundraisers for preschools, day-care centres, churches, and playgroups. For quantity discount information, write to us at the address below.

ORDER FORM

NUMBER OF COPIES		TOTAL
_____	***Surviving Your Toddler***, at $18.95	_____
_____	***Surviving Your Preschooler***, at $18.95	_____
	Postage and Handling, $3.00 per book	_____
	Subtotal	_____
	GST (7% of Subtotal)	_____
	Total Enclosed	_____

Please make your cheque or money order payable in Canadian funds to:
Lighthouse Books, 1423 Dayton Street,
Coquitlam, British Columbia, V3E 3H2, (604) 944-9622

SEND BOOKS TO: *(please print)*

Name:_____

Address: _____

City: _____ Province: _____

Postal Code: _____

Watch for *Picture Book Activities for Preschoolers*, available in the Fall of 2000